365 Words Every Kid Should Know

Lauren Holowaty
Martina Motzo

16pt

Copyright Page from the Original Book

First published in Great Britain in 2020 by Buster Books,
an imprint of Michael O'Mara Books Limited,
9 Lion Yard, Tremadoc Road, London SW4 7NQ

W www.mombooks.com/buster
f Buster Books
@BusterBooks

Copyright © Buster Books 2020

All rights reserved. No part of this publication may be reproduced, stored in a retrieval system, or transmitted by any means, without the prior permission in writing of the publisher, nor be otherwise circulated in any form of binding or cover other than that in which it is published and without a similar condition including this condition being imposed on the subsequent purchaser.

A CIP catalogue record for this book is available from the British Library.

2 4 6 8 10 9 7 5 3 1

Printed and bound in August 2020 by CPI Group (UK) Ltd,
108 Beddington Lane, Croydon, CR0 4YY, United Kingdom

TABLE OF CONTENTS

INTRODUCTION	iii
OUR WORLD	1
FOOD & DRINK	15
GOOD, BAD & UGLY	27
GET SPORTY	34
TALKING POLITICS	41
THE UK v THE USA	52
FAMILIAR FEELINGS	61
LET'S TALK	67
THIS ONE OR THAT ONE?	83
BOO!	109
BORROWED LANGUAGE	117
YOUR HISTORY	129
MUSIC TIME	140
WORDS OF ART	154
BOOK TALK	160
PERFECT PREFIXES	169
IN SICKNESS & IN HEALTH	188
MONEY, MONEY, MONEY	200
WEATHER WORDS	210
BY THE NUMBERS	221
ARE THEY EVEN REAL WORDS?	233
TOUGH TO SPELL	245
EXTRA TOUGH TO SPELL	261
WOW WORDS	277
Index	289

TABLE OF CONTENTS

INTRODUCTION	iii
OUR WORLD	1
FOOD & DRINK	15
GOOD, BAD & UGLY	27
GET SHORTY	34
TALKING POLITICS	41
THE U.K. v. THE USA	52
FAMILIAR FEELINGS	61
LET'S TALK	73
THIS ONE OR THAT ONE	83
BOO!	109
BORROWED LANGUAGE	117
YOUR HISTORY	129
MUSIC TIME	141
WORDS OF ART	154
BOOK TALK	160
PERFECT PREFIXES	169
IN SICKNESS & IN HEALTH	188
MONEY MONEY MONEY	200
WEATHER WORDS	210
BY THE NUMBERS	221
ARE THEY EVEN REAL WORDS?	238
TOUGH TO SPELL	245
EXTRA-TOUGH TO SPELL	251
WOW WORDS	277
Index	289

WRITTEN BY LAUREN HOLOWATY

ILLUSTRATED BY MARTINA MOTZO

EDITED BY GARY PANTON

DESIGNED BY ZOE BRADLEY

COVER DESIGNED BY JOHN BIGWOOD

EDUCATIONAL CONSULTATION BY KIRSTIN SWANSON

THANKS TO CLAIRE & KIMBERLEY DAVIS AT LITTLE OWL

WRITTEN BY LAUREN HOLOWATY

ILLUSTRATED BY MARTINA MOTZO

EDITED BY GARY PANTON

DESIGNED BY TOM BRADLEY

COVER DESIGNED BY JOHN BIGWOOD

EDUCATIONAL CONSULTATION BY
KRISTIN SWANSON

THANKS TO CLAIRE & KIMBERLEY
DAVIS AT STEM.ORG

INTRODUCTION

Did you know that there are over 250,000 words in the English language?

In this book you are going to find out about 365 words that every kid should know. That's one word a day for an entire year.

Each word has been specially selected to help you understand how it's spelled, where it comes from, or simply just what it means. Also included are handy example sentences so that you can be confident you're using your new-found favourite words in the right way.

These are words that can be used while you're at school, with family or hanging out with your friends. You can use them absolutely anywhere! Whether you're into history, sport, music, art or pretty much anything else, there's something for you in here.

So, what are you waiting for? It's time to get word wise!

OUR WORLD

Words about our planet, our environment and the natural world.

ENVIRONMENT

Your personal *environment* is everything surrounding you that has an effect on you. It includes the place you live, the people you see and the things that happen to you in your life. When people talk about the *environment*, they're normally referring to the natural world. This includes, for example, all of the planet's seas, land, plants and creatures.

Spellcheck

Remember the n in *environment*. You don't usually hear it when you say the word, but if you think of the *environment* as being 'nature' you should remember to add the *n*.

POLLUTION

When a substance is introduced into the natural world that causes harm to the environment, it is called *pollution*. Water, air and land can all suffer the effects of *pollution* from dirty, poisonous chemicals and waste.

Other uses

It's not just the environment that can be *polluted*.

Anything that has been damaged or corrupted can be said to have been *polluted*, too. A person who has become negatively influenced by money might be described as having been *polluted by greed*.

ATMOSPHERE

Have you ever looked up and wondered what all that emptiness around our planet is? It might look like there's nothing there at all – just lots and lots of space. Actually, there is a layer of gases surrounding Earth, called the *atmosphere*.

Something in the air

If you want to really impress people, you could learn the specific gases that make up our *atmosphere*. The main ones are:

- nitrogen (78%)
- oxygen (21%)
- argon (0.93%)
- carbon dioxide (0.04%).

Plus there are tiny traces of neon, helium, methane, krypton, hydrogen and water vapour.

Other uses

Atmosphere can also mean the feeling or mood you get from a place. A welcoming home might be said to have a *warm atmosphere*, while a haunted house would probably have a *spooky atmosphere*.

Did you know?
Mercury has the thinnest *atmosphere* of all the planets in our solar system.

POLE

You've probably heard of a certain someone coming from the *North Pole* to deliver gifts to children at Christmas time. And you'll also know that at the opposite end of the planet lies the *South Pole*. But do you know what the Earth's *poles* actually are? In geography, they are the most northern and southern parts of the globe. Earth also has *magnetic poles*, which are in different locations from the *geographic poles*. The *magnetic poles* are what compasses use to find north and south.

Other uses

A *pole* is also a long, thin piece of wood or metal. A *Pole*, with a capital *p*, might refer to a person from the country of Poland.

Not to be confused with...

Poll (an election or survey used to find out people's opinions on something). Despite the spelling, *poll* is pronounced the same way as *pole*.

Did you know?

The phrase *poles apart* is sometimes used to describe two people who have nothing in common with each other.

EQUATOR

The *equator* is the invisible line that separates the top half of the Earth, known as the northern hemisphere, from the bottom half, known as the southern hemisphere. The *equator* is the same distance from the geographic North Pole (at the top of the Earth) as it is from the geographic South Pole (at the bottom), and goes all the way round the planet.

Where does it come from?

The word *equator* comes from the Latin aequāre, meaning 'to make equal'. All spheres have an *equator,* but the word is mainly used when talking about Earth.

TROPIC

Planet Earth has two *tropics:* the *Tropic of Cancer* (to the north of the equator) and the *Tropic of Capricorn* (to the south). They are invisible lines, known as lines of latitude, that circle around the Earth.

Other uses

Tropic can also be short for *tropical*. People often use *tropical* as a general term for any hot weather, but it actually refers to the hot, damp weather associated with *the tropics*. *The tropics* are the regions that lie between the *Tropic of Cancer* and the *Tropic of Capricorn*.

CONTINENT

A *continent* is a large area of land, normally made up of several countries. The seven *continents* of the world are Africa, Antarctica, Asia, Australia, Europe, North America and South America.

Other uses

Strangely, *continent* also means being able to control when you wee and poo. If you are *incontinent*, you can't control these and might have an accident!

Did you know?

Antarctica (in the south) is considered a *continent*, but the Arctic (in the north) is not. That is because no single landmass makes up the Arctic as it does in Antarctica – the North Pole is actually sea covered in constantly moving ice.

ISLAND

Land that is surrounded by water is called an *island*. A *desert island*, despite the name, is normally a *tropical island* rather than one covered in desert. The phrase may come from the fact that desert *islands* are often deserted (as in, there's no one on them).

Silence please

When you say *island* the *s* is silent (meaning you see it, but don't say it). Remember: an *island* **is land.**

FOREIGN

If a person is *foreign*, it means that they come from a country other than your own. *Foreign* comes from the Latin word *foris*, meaning 'outside'. Always consider: someone might be *foreign* to you, but you're *foreign* to lots of other people, too.

Other uses

If something is *foreign* to someone, it can mean it is unknown, strange or unfamiliar to them.

Silence please

The g in *foreign* is silent, so *foreign* is pronounced 'faw-ruhn'.

Rule breaker

You might have been taught the rule '*i* before *e*, except after *c*'. Well, as you can see, *foreign* breaks this rule, like lots of words in the English language. Can you think of any others? Take a peek at the bottom of this page for some examples.

HORIZON

The *horizon* is where it appears that the sky meets the land (or the sea). If you're especially high up, such as when you're flying in an aeroplane, you may even be able to see the *horizon* as a curve. The *horizon* is curved because the Earth is curved.

> ### Did you know?
> *Broadening your horizons* means increasing your knowledge, taking on new things and trying out new experiences.

Rule breakers: beings, eight, feisty, forfeit, height, leisure, protein, species, their, weigh, weird.

STATE

This word has a lot of different meanings. In fact, it has too many to state in this book! A *state* can be a country, or divided-up regions within a country (such as the 50 different *states* of the *United States of America*). A government can also be referred to as *the state*. The person in charge of a country is often called the *Head of State*, and when that person travels to another country on official duty it's called a *state visit*.

Other uses

If you *state* something, you're saying it in a clear and definite way. State can also be used to describe the condition something is in. For example, *Look at the state of that building – it looks like it hasn't been painted in years.* You might also use the word *state* in science classes, to describe a chemical reaction that changes a substance's structure. For example, *Its state changed from a solid to a liquid.*

ORGANIC

If something is *organic*, it means that it grows naturally. So, why is some food considered *organic*, and some isn't? Well, *organic* food has been produced without the use of any pesticides or chemicals. Pesticides are used to kill bugs and insects that harm plants, but insects are an important part of the natural world. Harming insects also harms the environment.

RECYCLABLE

Things such as paper, aluminium cans and glass bottles are *recyclable*, which means that once they have been used, they can be made into something else that can also be used.

Recyclable v reusable

You've probably *recycled* much of your rubbish before, but you could also try reusing some of it. *Recycling* a plastic bottle is good for the environment, but it's not perfect, because it has to go through a process that uses energy. Simply reusing your bottle instead would be even better. All you have to do is hold on to it, wash it out and refill it!

RENEWABLE

If you've ever borrowed books from a library before, you'll already know the word *renew* – it means you can take your books home again and again. In the natural world, *renewable* resources are things like water, sunlight and wind. Not only can they be used to generate energy, but they can be used over and over again – just like your library books.

Break it down

If you break the word down it's easy to remember. Something that is *renewable* is *able* to be *renewed*.

SUSTAINABLE

Something that is *sustainable* can be continued at the same rate without any problems. Solar energy, for example, is a *sustainable* energy source. It can be collected from the Sun's rays without using anything up or causing damage to the planet.

Other uses

A person's whole lifestyle could be *sustainable*. This means they live in a way that only uses *sustainable* resources. When a whole group of people live this way, it's called a *sustainable society*.

BIODEGRADABLE

If something is *biodegradable*, it decays naturally. Lots of coffee shops, for example, now use *biodegradable* paper cups instead of plastic ones. *Biodegradable* materials are good news for the planet, because they don't need any help from chemicals to break down, so they don't cause pollution. The *bio* part of the word in this case comes from the Greek *bios,* meaning 'life'.

GEOTHERMAL

Heat that comes from beneath the Earth's surface is referred to as *geothermal* (with *geo* meaning the Earth, and *thermal* relating to heat). A *geothermal* heat pump is able to take this energy from the ground and use it to heat our homes. Clever, huh?

Did you know?

14

> Some cities in the United States use pipes to channel *geothermal* hot water underneath roads and paths to melt snow.

FOOD & DRINK

Words to get you salivating. [1]

RESTAURANT

A *restaurant* is a place where people go to eat and pay for a meal. The meals are usually cooked by a chef, and served to the tables by a waiter or waitress.

Where does it come from?

Restaurant originally comes from the French word *restaurer*, which means 'restore'. This is because, at one time, *restaurants* in France boasted that their food would 'restore' your health. A person who runs a restaurant is called a *restaurateur* (with no *n*). Confusingly, you can also get away with keeping the *n* in and saying *restauranteur*. Maybe just call them the *restaurant owner* and make it easy!

DIET

Your *diet* is the food you normally eat each day. If you eat a wide range of healthy food such as fruit and vegetables as well as other kinds of

---

[1] That means your mouth is watering!

food like rice and beans, it's called having a *balanced diet*.

Other uses

If you are *on a diet*, it means you are changing the food you eat to improve your health.

BALANCED DIET

VEGETABLE

A plant that you can cook and eat — such as a potato, leek or carrot — is called a *vegetable*.

Vegetable v fruit

Telling the difference between *vegetables* and fruit can be tricky. Technically, if it has seeds and comes from a flowering plant, then it's a fruit. Anything else you eat that is part of a plant (including roots and stems) is a *vegetable*. So, because they have seeds, tomatoes are actually a kind of fruit!

VEGAN

Someone who doesn't eat any meat, fish or other animal products is a *vegan*.

Vegan v vegetarian

The words *vegan* and vegetarian sound similar, but they mean different things. A vegetarian does not eat meat or fish, but will eat other animal products such as eggs, cheese, butter and milk. A *vegan* doesn't eat any of these things.

But why?

There are lots of different reasons why a person might choose to be either *vegan* or vegetarian. Some do it for health reasons, some do it for environmental reasons, and some do it simply because they don't like the idea of eating animals. Some people also disagree with eating certain types of meat because of their religious beliefs.

PESCATARIAN

Someone who eats fish but not any other kind of meat is a *pescatarian*. The *pesc* part of the word comes from *pesce*, which means 'fish' in Italian.

Spellcheck

This is one of those annoying words that has two acceptable spellings. While *pescatarian*, with an a in the middle, is the most common spelling, it's also OK to spell it with a second e, as *pescetarian*.

CURRANT

Currants are small black fruit made from dried seedless grapes. They are often used in baking. You may have tried a *currant bun* before, or a fruitcake with *currants* in it. Yum! You might also have heard of raisins and sultanas (which are also known as golden raisins). These can all taste pretty similar, but the difference comes from the type of grape that has been used to make them.

Not to be confused with...

Current (a flow or movement, often of either water or electricity). *Current* can also mean now, as in *It is currently 3pm so it's nearly home time!*

ROAST

When you *roast* food, you cook it in an oven or fire. A *roast dinner* is sometimes referred to as simply a roast.

Roasting v boiling (and frying and grilling!)

All of these are different techniques for cooking food. When you boil food, you submerge it in boiling water. Frying involves placing food into oil that has been heated from below. Grilling can involve heat from either above or below, but doesn't require oil.

Other uses

If a person is really hot, for example on a summer's day at the beach, they might say they are *roasting* or boiling. It's unlikely that they'd say they are frying or grilling, though.

And...

A *roast* is also an event at which a person has jokes told about them in public.

BARBECUE

A *barbecue* is an event, a type of cooking and also the piece of equipment used to do that cooking. It's quite confusing, but it also makes it easy in a way as it means there's only one word to learn! A *barbecue* usually happens outdoors, and the food is cooked either over an open fire or on a *barbecue* itself.

Saucy

Barbecue sauce is a sweet, smoky-flavoured sauce often served with food that has been *barbecued*.

Spellcheck

Barbecue can also be spelled as *barbeque*, and you might also see it written as *Bar-B-Q* or even just *BBQ*. In Australia and New Zealand, it's often shortened to *barbie*.

GRATE

Here's a *great*[2] example of a word with multiple uses. Check out the top three:

1. You may have come across *grate* in recipes. In this case, it means to shred into small pieces. Things that commonly get *grated* include cheese and carrots (and occasionally knuckles and fingers, which is why it's wise to be careful when *grating*).
2. If something *grates on you*, it means that it annoys you. For example, you could say it *grates on you* when one word means loads of different things.

---

[2] Note the different spelling.

3. The metal bars that go across the front of a fireplace to hold in the wood or coal are also called a *grate*.

Not to be confused with...

Great (meaning very large, very important, very good or very impressive). Great is also used to describe a person who is older or younger by one generation (such as a *great-grandfather* or *great-granddaughter*).

DOUGH

Bread, pastry and pizza bases are made with a thick mixture of flour and liquid called *dough*.

Other uses

    Dough is also a slang term for money, as in, *Emma won the lottery and now she has lots of dough!*

Spellcheck

Dough is spelled the same way as 'cough', but it's pronounced 'doe'.

Not to be confused with...

Doe (a female deer) or *doh* (which you might say after making a mistake).

KNEAD

You *knead* something by pressing and stretching it with your hands. Dough is often *kneaded* to make it ready for baking.

Not to be confused with...

Need (when something is required – for example, you *need* to breathe oxygen in order to live).

SPAGHETTI

Spaghetti is a type of pasta that comes in long, stringy strips that you have to wind round your fork. *Spaghetti* can be served in lots of ways, such as with meatballs or bolognese sauce. Eating *spaghetti* without getting the sauce all over your face and clothes can be quite a skill!

Where does it come from?

Spaghetti is an Italian food, so it makes sense that it is also an Italian word. In Italian, *spaghetti* is the plural of *spago*, which means 'string'. *Spaghetti* is pronounced 'spah-geh-tee'.

UMAMI

There are said to be five basic types of taste in food: salty, sweet, sour, bitter and *umami*.

Umami is a savoury taste that is very difficult to describe. Foods that are naturally high in *umami* are not sweet, including soy sauce, black olives, fish, beef, parmesan cheese and tomatoes.

Where does it come from?

Umami is a Japanese word that means 'deliciousness'. Sounds pretty good, right?

GOOD, BAD & UGLY

Words to use when things are going well ... or not so well.

WICKED

If someone is *wicked*, then they are evil, very bad or cruel. For example, *The wicked witch wanted to turn the children into mice.* Occasionally it is used in a more playful way to describe someone as cheeky or mischievous. For example, *Cleo has a wicked sense of fun. She loves playing practical jokes on people.*

Other uses

Confusingly, *wicked* can also mean excellent, as in *We went skiing and had a wicked time!* This way of using *wicked* started out as slang, but has become increasingly normal.

MISCHIEVOUS

When someone causes trouble or is naughty in a playful way, they are said to be *mischievous*.

Spellcheck

Although *mischievous* is sometimes incorrectly pronounced 'mis-chee-vee-ous', there is no extra *i* after the *v*. Think of *mischievous* as like *mischief*, but with the same ending as 'nervous' – so 'mis-chif-us'. It might help to remember it this way: *The mischievous boy is chiefly nervous.*

NUISANCE

A *nuisance* is anyone or anything that causes problems or annoyance. You might call someone who bugs you a *nuisance*.

Spellcheck

Keep an eye on the *s* and *c* in *nuisance*, as they're easy to get the wrong way round. Try thinking of it this way: the fact that they don't appear in alphabetical order is a *nuisance*. *Nuisance* is pronounced 'new-suhns'.

MARVELLOUS

Something that is *marvellous* is wonderful, extraordinary and a complete and utter *marvel*. Other words that are similar in meaning include fantastic, grand, great, terrific and tremendous.

Where does it come from?

Marvellous comes from the Old French word *merveille*, which became *marvel* in English.

EXCELLENT

If something is *excellent*, it is really very good. It's *excellent* that you are reading this, as you will be able to use the word *excellent* from now on. Keep up the *excellent* work.

Spellcheck

Don't forget the *c* in the middle. It may help if you try to remember that *you can count on an excellent person*.

DISASTROUS

A *disaster* is an incredibly bad event, and something that causes a *disaster* to happen is *disastrous*. *Disastrous* events often involve tragedy and devastation, such as a volcanic eruption, earthquake or tsunami.

TRIVIAL

Something *trivial* is unimportant or insignificant. For example, *The teacher asked not to be bothered with trivial questions.* You might have heard of a *trivia game*. This is usually a quiz where players are asked questions about subjects that are interesting, but not very important.

INSIPID

If you find something distasteful, dull or boring, you might call it *insipid*. The word is sometimes used to describe food that is lacking in flavour. A boring movie could also be described as *insipid*.

Where does it come from?

Insipid derives from Latin, where *sapidus* means 'full of flavour', so *insipidus* means the exact opposite.

APPRECIATE

If you value something or recognize how much something is worth, you *appreciate* it.

Other uses

Appreciate can mean the same as 'understand'. For example, *Yusuf appreciated that he would only win the race if he trained hard.* *Appreciate* can also mean that the cost of something has gone up. *The house's value was appreciating over time.*

Spellcheck

Notice that *appreciate* starts with a double *p*, just like an app you would download on your phone or tablet. The *c* makes a 'sh' sound, so the word is pronounced 'ah-pree-shee-ate'.

PHENOMENAL

Something amazing or extraordinary can be described as *phenomenal*. For example, *The atmosphere in the stadium when Charlie's team won the game was phenomenal.*

> ### Did you know?
> A *phenomenon* is something that exists but seems remarkable or unusual. *Phenomenon* can also be used to describe something that

suddenly becomes hugely popular. For example, you could say, *Clara's band was a phenomenon.*

AGGRESSIVE

If someone is *aggressive*, they are likely to be angry and hostile. If you know of someone who is often getting into fights, it may be because they are *aggressive*.

Why the aggro?

Aggro is a slang term that is short for *aggressive*. It can also be used to describe the problems that are putting you off doing an unappealing task. For example, *Darius didn't mow the lawn because he didn't want the aggro.*

CONTROVERSY

A long or big disagreement or argument is called a *controversy*. It might also be called a *controversy* when someone does something that causes other people to become angry. Such an act would be described as *controversial* (pronounced 'kon-troh-ver-shal').

Where does it come from?

Controversy comes from the Latin contrōversus, which means 'turned in an opposite direction'. *Contra* means 'against', which you can also see in the word 'contradict'. If you contradict someone, you say the opposite thing to what they have said.

GET SPORTY

Words for keeping fit with.

OLYMPICS

Every four years, a different city from around the world hosts a huge sporting event called the *Olympic Games*. The Games as we know them (the *modern Olympics*) were first held in 1896, but the original Games (the *ancient Olympics*) date all the way back to ancient Greece. Since 1924, there have been *Winter Olympics* too, which are also held every four years.

Where does it come from?

The word *Olympics* comes from *Olympia* – an ancient town in Greece where the games originally took place. A person who takes part in the *Olympics* is called an *Olympian*.

PARALYMPICS

The *Paralympics* is a sporting event that runs alongside the *Olympic Games*. It was originally just for people who had fought in World War II, but is now open to any athlete with a disability.

Where does it come from?

It's sometimes mistakenly thought that the *para* part comes from 'paraplegic' (a person unable to move the lower half of their body). In fact, *para* comes from the fact that the games run 'parallel' to the Olympics.

MARATHON

A *marathon* is a very long running race – 42.2 kilometres long, to be exact. *Marathons* are run all over the world, with particularly famous ones in London, Boston and New York. Competitors in *marathons* can range from professional athletes to complete beginners raising money for charities. Some people even run *marathons* in fancy dress. Back in 2002, a man took part in the *London Marathon* wearing a heavy deep-sea diving suit. It took him more than five whole days to complete the race!

Where does it come from?

Just like 'Olympics', the word *marathon* comes from a place in Greece. Legend has it that an ancient Greek messenger ran about 40 kilometres from *Marathon* to Athens to deliver news of a war victory. That story inspired the races that still take place today.

HEPTATHLON

A *heptathlon* is a sporting contest made up of seven different events. The events are: long jump, high jump, javelin, shot put, 200-metre race, 800-metre race and 100-metre hurdles.

Where does it come from?

Hepta means 'seven' and *athlon* means 'contest'.

DECATHLON

A *decathlon* involves a whopping ten different events. They are: pole vault, long jump, high jump, discus, javelin, shot put, 1,500-metre race, 400-metre race, 100-metre race and 110-metre hurdles.

Where does it come from?

Deca means 'ten' and *athlon* (just like with 'heptathlon') means 'contest'.

COMPETITION

A *competition* is any event where people try to win against each other. *Competition* often applies to sport, but you can have all sorts of *competitions*, from cooking to maths or science. People who take part in *competitions* are called *competitors*, and the ones who take them extra-seriously might be described as *competitive*.

TACTICS

Tactics are the methods people use in a competition to try to win. For example, a runner might decide to hang back and save their energy in a race, before bursting into a sprint at the end. Or a soccer coach might tell their team to pass the ball to their fastest player. *Tactics* are used outside sport, too. You might even use them in a video game or board game.

TROPHY

A *trophy* is any sort of reward, such as a cup or medal, that you might receive after winning something. Successful sports clubs often have *trophy cabinets* where they put all their *trophies* to show them off.

DRIBBLE

In team sports involving a round ball (such as basketball or soccer), *dribbling* is where a player keeps the ball to themselves and runs with it to get past members of the other team.

Other uses

A *dribble* can also mean a slow flow of water. If a person is *dribbling*, and there's no ball in sight, it usually means they have spit running from their mouth!

dribbling / DRIBBLING

AEROBIC

In biology, *aerobic* means 'with oxygen'. Exercise that gets your heart pumping and strengthens your lungs (such as running or cycling) is called *aerobic* exercise. Some people go to *aerobic classes* (often shortened to just *aerobics*), where they do *aerobic* exercises in a group with a teacher.

The science part

By making your heart work harder, *aerobic* exercise helps your body absorb and transport oxygen. This extra workout for your heart is called 'cardiovascular activity', or 'cardio' for short.

Just the opposite

The opposite of *aerobic* is *anaerobic*. Anaerobic exercise doesn't raise your heart rate, but it improves your strength by using short, sudden bursts of energy. An example of *anaerobic* exercise is weightlifting.

TALKING POLITICS

Words about how things are run.

GOVERNMENT

The group of people who are in charge of a country are its *government*. Some *governments* are voted into their position by the people, while others seize power for themselves. *Governments* can be lead by a president, a prime minister, a king or a queen, but they all have one thing in common: they tell us what we can and cannot do.

Spellcheck

Watch out for the *n* in the middle of *government*. You can hear it in *govern*, *governing* and *governor*, but you may not hear it in the pronunciation of *government*.

ELECTION

An *election* is a contest in which people vote to choose who should have a particular job. *Elections* are often held to select a political leader, but they can happen for all sorts of reasons. You might even have an *election* at your school to choose student reps or prefects.

Other uses

Election can mean making a choice in general, and doesn't always have to refer to voting. For example, you might say, *I have elected to stop using plastic bottles.*

And the winner is...

Deciding on the winner of an *election* might seem simple. The person with the most votes wins, right? Well, yes, but it can be a little more complicated than that. Imagine a scenario where the most popular candidate only gains 40% of the votes. They have more votes than anyone else, but it means that 60% of the voters wanted other candidates. In countries using the system known as 'first past the post', that person would be declared the winner. In countries using the 'proportional representation' system, that person would still win, but they would only get 40% of the seats in parliament. Some countries insist that the winner must have over 50% of the votes, so would hold a second round of voting involving the top candidates. That means the same number of votes could result in completely different outcomes when different voting systems are used.

REFERENDUM

A *referendum* is similar to an election in that it's a public vote, but a *referendum* is held to answer a question rather than elect a person. When a particularly big issue comes along, the government might choose to let the people decide by holding a *referendum*.

DEMOCRACY

A *democracy* is a political system in which the people in a country choose who they would like to represent them in government. Typically, politicians are elected into their positions to represent the people who live in their local area. The politicians then vote among themselves to make decisions.

DICTATORSHIP

A *dictatorship* is the opposite of a democracy. In a *dictatorship,* one person (known as a *dictator*) or one political party makes all the decisions without consulting the people. In some cases, there can be frightening consequences for saying anything that criticizes or disagrees with the *dictator*.

Other uses

To *dictate* basically means to say something aloud and tell someone else what to do. *Dictators* do this, but it can also refer to speaking or reading something out loud while someone else writes it down. A secretary typing out someone else's spoken words is *taking dictation*.

CAMPAIGN

A *campaign* is an organized attempt to change or achieve something. A *political campaign* is when people try to persuade others to vote for them in an election.

Other uses

If you *campaign* for a change, you're trying to change someone's mind in order to get your way. You'll also have seen *advertising campaigns*, which try to convince you to buy a particular product.

Spellcheck

Campaign is a real *paign* (pain) to spell. To remember the g in the middle, try thinking of this phrase: *a campaign is all about getting your way.*

CANVASS

In the run-up to an election you may see politicians *canvassing*. This means they are going around an area trying to persuade people to vote for a certain person or party. You can also *canvass* opinion. This is where you find out how people feel about a particular subject.

Not to be confused with...

Canvas (a board used for painting on, or the cloth material sometimes used for bags).

COUP

A *coup* is when a group of people seize power from their government, often very suddenly and violently. *Coup* is short for *coup d'état* (pronounced 'koo deh tah'). The unusual spelling is because it's a French term. A *military coup* is where members of the armed forces (such as the army, navy or air force) take charge of how their country is run.

Did you know?

Be careful if you ever say *coup* in Scotland. There, they also say *coo* – which means 'cow'!

LOBBY

A *lobby* is a group of people who stick up for a certain idea, issue or organization, and try to convince the government to help them. If you *lobby* a politician, it means you're trying to persuade them that something needs to be done, or a law needs to be changed.

Other uses

A *lobby* is also the name for the area just inside the entrance to a large building such as a hotel or museum.

GUERRILLA

A *guerrilla* is someone in an unofficial army who fights against a country's official army or police. *Guerrilla fighters* are often trying to overthrow the government and gain control, as part of a coup.

Where does it come from?

The word *guerrilla* comes from the Spanish word *guerra,* meaning 'war'.

Other uses

If you do anything without permission, you might be a *guerrilla* too! *Guerrilla gardeners,* for example, are people who create gardens on sites that don't belong to them.

Not to be confused with...

Guerrilla is pronounced the same way as gorilla, but the two are very different!

COMMUNITY

A *community* can be any group of people who share something in common. The people who live in your neighbourhood are your local *community*. However, a *community* doesn't have to be about location. For example, people who run businesses are often called the *business community*, and people who go to schools or colleges are the *student community*.

That's the spirit

When people are enthusiastic about making things better in their local area, it's called having a *community spirit*. Acts of *community spirit* can range from doing volunteer work to picking up litter.

COMMUNITY SPIRIT

ECONOMY

Economy normally refers to money and how it moves around a region. If a country has a thriving *economy*, it means it's doing very well for itself.

Other uses

You've probably seen *economy packs* of things such as toilet rolls or batteries. These are bulk packs of objects that would cost a lot more if you bought them on their own, so you're saving money by buying them together.

Watch out!

If you are being *economical*, you're good at saving money. But if you're being *economical with the truth*, it may mean you're a fibber!

COMMITTEE

A *committee* is a group of people who get together to make decisions, plans and reports. You can get *committees* for all sorts of things, from village sports teams right up to the highest levels of government. Some *committees* organize events, while others investigate wrongs and make recommendations. In politics, *committees* tend to be busily working in the background, keeping an eye on things such as policy and spending.

Spellcheck

Remember: a *committee* is made up of more than one person, and also has lots of double letters. Two *m*'s, two *t*'s, two *e*'s!

COUNCIL

A *council* is a group of people who meet to discuss issues and make decisions, often about their local area. In politics, the members of a *council* are *councillors*, who have often been chosen through an election.

Not to be confused with...

Counsel (advice). Remember, while a *councillor* is someone who is a member of a *council*, a *counsellor* is someone who gives advice and helps people with their personal problems. It may help to remember it this way: *a counsellor gives support.*

Council v committee

This is where it can get confusing. A *council* and a committee can seem very similar, and the words are often used to mean the same thing. However, as a general rule, a *council* is normally more senior than a committee. A *council* might set up a committee to look into a specific issue, but it would never happen the other way round.

THE UK v THE USA

Words that are spelled differently on one side of the Atlantic from the other.

CENTRE or CENTER

The *centre* of something is its middle. For example, *Tim stood in the centre of the room while everyone sang Happy Birthday to him.* If someone is the *centre of attention,* they are the main focus of everyone else in the room.

Other uses

A *centre* can also be a building where people meet. A *community centre* is one example. A *town centre* or *city centre* isn't necessarily right in the middle, but it is generally where most of the shops and businesses are.

The UK v the USA

When the er sound is at the end of a word, the UK usually uses *re* while the United States uses *er*. Other examples of this are: theatre (theater), and the units of measurement litre (liter) and metre (meter).

PROGRAMME or PROGRAM

A *programme* is a plan of events, a TV or radio show, or even a little booklet you are given when you go to an event such as a play or a concert. You can *programme* something like a robot, a machine, a system or your TV so you can watch your favourite *programme*. You could even *programme* your robot to *programme* your TV to show all your favourite *programmes*! The question is: is your brain *programmed* to take this much *programming*?

The UK v the USA

Most of the time, the UK uses *programme*. Sometimes, the Brits use *program* when talking about computers, but either spelling is acceptable in that context. In the US, it's much simpler: they just use *program* for everything.

AEROPLANE or AIRPLANE

You probably already know what an *aeroplane* is. It's that vehicle with wings and an engine that flies through the sky from one place to another. But have you ever noticed that in the UK it's called an *aeroplane*, while in the US it's called an *airplane*?

The UK v the USA

Aero, as used in the UK, comes from Greek and relates to the air or atmosphere. In the US, they've replaced this first part of the word with *air*. The *plane* part comes from the Greek word *planos*, which means 'wandering'.

JEWELLERY or JEWELRY

Rings, necklaces, bracelets and earrings are all types of personal ornaments known as *jewellery*. *Jewellery* tends to be made of metals such as gold or silver and often has precious stones in it. In prehistoric times, shells and animal teeth were used instead.

The UK v the USA

The UK and USA agree on the spelling of *jewel*, but then it gets a little more confusing. In the UK they add *lery* on to the end, while the Americans add *ry*.

OFFENCE or OFFENSE

An *offence* is something that is wrong or against the law, such as a crime. Stealing is an example of a *criminal offence*. *Offence* can also be a feeling of hurt or annoyance. For example, *Jacob took offence when Ayesha said she didn't like his drawings.*

The UK v the USA

In the UK, it's spelled *offence*, while in the US it's *offense*. Other words that share this difference in spelling include defence (defense). However, both the UK and USA use an s in the word *offensive*.

Attack or offense?

In the US, *offense* is often used as a sports term, whereas in the UK the word 'attack' is more common.

TRAVELLER or TRAVELER

Someone who moves around or travels is called a *traveller*.

The UK v the USA

In the UK, they tend to double the *l* at the end of a word when adding suffixes (that means extra bits like 'er', 'ing' and 'ed'). So, while *travel* becomes *traveler* in America, in the UK it becomes *traveller*. Some similar examples of this are: cancelled (canceled), modelling (modeling) and fuelled (fueled).

PYJAMAS or PAJAMAS

Pyjamas – also known as *PJs, jim-jams* and *jammies* – are loose clothes designed to be worn in bed.

Where does it come from?

Pyjamas comes from two Urdu and Persian words: pāi, meaning 'leg', and jāmah, which means 'clothing'.

The UK v the USA

In the UK, it's spelled *pyjamas*, while in the US it's *pajamas*. One way to remember this might be to think of the A for *America* also being the extra a in *pajamas*.

MANOEUVRE or MANEUVER

To *manoeuvre* something is to skilfully move it around or into place. *Will carefully manoeuvred his bike round the obstacle course.*

Where does it come from?

Manoeuvre comes from the Latin manū operāre, referring to manual work or simply 'to work with the hand'.

The UK v the USA

This is one of the toughest words to spell, even without the differences! It's *manoeuvre* in the UK and *maneuver* in the US, but it's always pronounced 'man-oo-vur'.

DIALOGUE or DIALOG

Dialogue is the conversation between people in a play, film or book. You can also have a *dialogue* with someone in real life, which simply means to have a conversation with them.

The UK v the USA

In the UK, it's *dialogue* and in America it's *dialog*, but the pronunciation is always the same: 'die-ah-log'.

LICENCE or LICENSE

A *licence* gives you permission to do something. For example, a *driving* licence gives you permission to drive a car.

The UK v the USA

In the US, this word is always spelled *license*, with an s. However, in the UK it's spelled as *licence* when it's a noun but *license* when it's a verb. So you'd be correct to write *I have a pilot's* licence, but you'd also be correct to write *I am licensed to be a pilot*. It may help to remember that the s in *license* is near the end of the alphabet, just like v for 'verb'.

PRACTISE or PRACTICE

When you *practise* something, you do it over and over again to get better at it.

The UK v the USA

In the USA, this one's simple: they use *practice* for everything. In the UK, it's more complicated: *practise* is used for the verb (*Chloe practises the piano every evening*), and *practice* is used for the noun (*Practice makes perfect*).

Other uses

A *practice* can also be a business, such as a doctor's or lawyer's *practice*. When used as a noun in this way, it's spelled *practice* whether you're in the UK or US.

FAVOURITE or FAVORITE

If something is your *favourite*, it is the thing you like the absolute best. *Anya's favourite book was full of stories about dragons.*

The UK v the USA

Favourite is the British spelling, and *favorite* is the American. Other words where Brits use an our while Americans use an or include colour (color) and neighbour (neighbor).

FAMILIAR FEELINGS

Words about emotions.

APPREHENSIVE

When you are *apprehensive*, you feel worried, fearful or nervous that something bad might happen. *The baby turtle felt apprehensive about swimming in the ocean for the first time.*

Other uses

Apprehension can also relate to being captured. When the police make an arrest, they may say the criminal has been *apprehended*. *The burglar felt apprehensive about being apprehended.*

DESPERATE

If you are in a bad situation and will do whatever it takes to make things better, you could be described as *desperate*. If someone says they are feeling *desperate*, it could be that they are feeling hopeless and very sad. On the other hand, it could also mean that they badly need to wee!

Where does it come from?

Desperate is closely linked to the word *despair* and comes from the Latin word *desperatus*, meaning 'deprived of hope'. If you really need a wee, try not to lose hope!

Spellcheck

Remember, *desperate* has an **e** in the middle, just like the w**e**e you might be *desp**e**rate* for!

DETERMINED

If you are feeling *determined* about something, you have your mind made up and you're set on exactly what you want to do. For example, *Eva was determined to do a perfect cartwheel on the gymnastic beam by the end of the year.*

HYSTERICAL

If someone is laughing uncontrollably or is very excited, angry or panicky, they are said to be *hysterical*. Some celebrities and bands have fans who get so *hysterical* that they start screaming and crying. When a group of people act in this way, it's called *hysteria*.

Other uses

Something that is very funny could also be described as *hysterical*. For example, *That joke was hysterically funny*. If you are *in hysterics*, it means you are laughing a lot.

DEPRESSED

Being *depressed* means having a feeling of severe sadness and helplessness. *Depression* is a mental-health condition that can make it difficult to feel happy and enjoy life. Just like with other illnesses, *depression* is something that doctors can help with.

Other uses

If a surface is *depressed*, it means it has a dip in it. The economy can also become depressed. In an *economic depression*, lots of businesses close and many people lose their jobs.

CURIOUS

You know that feeling you get when you want to find out more about something? That's the feeling of *curiosity*. For example, *Tina was curious to find out what curiosity meant*. If you are *curious*, then you're interested, questioning or even just plain old nosy.

Spellcheck

For some *curious* reason (yes, *curious* can also mean 'strange'), curious has a second *u*, but curiosity doesn't.

> ### Did you know?
> The phrase *curiosity killed the cat* is sometimes used as a warning not to pry too much into other people's business, as it may backfire on you!

AWED

When you are *awed*, you have an intense feeling of wonder and amazement. You could be in *awe* of a beautiful view or a famous painting. If you are *awed* by a person, it means you respect and admire them so much that you are overwhelmed and possibly even a little scared. For example, *Layla was in awe of her favourite pop star.*

Not to be confused with...

Aw (as in, *Aw, look at the cute puppy* or *Aw, why can't I have some more chocolate?*)

PESSIMISTIC

If you are *pessimistic*, you have the feeling or belief that the worst thing is going to happen. People who think this way are called *pessimists*. For example, *Kamal was pessimistic about his football team's chances of winning their next game.*

Where does it come from?

Pessimistic comes from the Latin word *pessimus*, meaning 'worst'.

OPTIMISTIC

Optimistic is the opposite of pessimistic. *Optimism* is the belief that good things will happen and everything will work out well. For example, *Jane was optimistic that her football team could beat Kamal's.*

Where does it come from?

Optimistic comes from the Latin *optimus*, meaning 'best thing'. The English word *optimum*, meaning the best or highest level, comes from the same word.

Glass half full v glass half empty

A common way of describing the difference between *optimism* and pessimism is to refer to a glass that is filled halfway with water. An *optimist* would call the glass 'half full', while a pessimist would call the glass 'half empty'. Which one are you?

LET'S TALK

Words about getting your message across.

COMMUNICATE

To *communicate* means to exchange messages, feelings or information with someone else. You could *communicate* by speaking or writing, or by using body language or sign language. Scuba divers can't speak to each other underwater, so they use hand signals to *communicate*.

LANGUAGE

What you say, what you write and even what you are reading now is *language*. All methods of human communication involving sounds or symbols are referred to as *language*. English, which this book is written in, is just one example of the thousands of *languages* that are spoken all over the world.

> **Did you know?**
>
> Computers have *languages,* too. One of the most common is HTML, which stands for *hypertext markup language.* HTML is used to create the websites you probably look at every day.

EXPLAIN

To *explain* something is to help another person understand it, either by going into more detail or by making it simpler. For example, *The science teacher explained how to do the experiment.*

Other uses

Explaining can also mean giving a reason for something. For example, *Asim explained that he was late for school because he overslept.*

EXAGGERATE

If someone *exaggerates* something, they make it seem bigger, smaller, better or worse than it really is. For example, *Jasmine said she saw a dog as big as a house, but everyone knew she was exaggerating.*

Spellcheck

Don't *exaggerate* how difficult this word is to spell. It's not so hard, really. Just remember the double g, which is pronounced like a j.

INTERFERE

If you *interfere*, you get mixed up in something that doesn't involve you. For example, *Dad said it was best to let Rosie and Michael sort out their own disagreement and not to interfere.*

Other uses

When one thing *interferes* with another, it can mean that the first thing is getting in the way of the second thing happening. For example,

Ada was told that playing too many video games would interfere with her homework.

Spellcheck

Watch out for the last part of *interfere*. It's pronounced the same way as 'fear', but it's not spelled that way.

INTERRUPT

When you *interrupt* someone, you stop them from doing what they were in the process of doing. If someone was to talk to you while you were in the middle of reading this sentence, they would be guilty of *interrupting* you. If you have ever had someone talk over you while you're speaking, you'll know that being *interrupted* can be very annoying!

Spellcheck

Notice the double *r* in the middle of the word. Think of *interrupt* as being like two words smashed together: *inter* (meaning 'between') and *rupt* (short for 'rupture', meaning 'to break').

CRITICIZE

If you dislike something, you'll probably be tempted to *criticize* it. You *criticize* something by pointing out its flaws or weak spots. Normally, people don't like to be *criticized*, although it can be done in a positive way. *Constructive criticism* is when someone tells you what you have done wrong in a nice way, to help you to improve and do better next time.

Where does it come from?

Critic comes from the Latin *criticus*, which in turn comes from the Greek *kritikos*. The original meaning is 'capable of judging'. If you are criticizing something, you are judging it.

Did you know?

A person who *criticizes* things is called a *critic*. Some people even do this for a job. A *movie critic*, for example, watches movies and then gives their opinion on them.

HARASS

To *harass* someone is to bother or annoy them over and over again. A similar word is 'harry', which is now more commonly heard as a boy's name, but also means to pester a person. No one likes to be harried – not even people called Harry!

Where does it come from?

The word *harass* comes from the French *harer*, which means to order a dog to attack.

SUGGEST

To *suggest* is to put forward an idea. For example, *Theo suggested that everyone should go home early, but the teacher didn't like that suggestion.*

Other uses

You can also use *suggest* when one thing leads you to think of something else. For example, *The black clouds in the sky suggested a storm was coming.*

Spellcheck

Remember the double g in the middle. It's pronounced like a *j*, so you say the word as 'suh-jest'.

RECOMMEND

If you tell someone that something is good and they should try it out, you are *recommending* it. You might *recommend* a book, a movie or a place to play. You can even *recommend* a person. For example, *Andi's friend recommended her for the job.*

Where does it come from?

Recommend comes from the Latin commendā re, which means 'to commend'. In English, if you 'commend' someone you give them praise.

EAVESDROP

To *eavesdrop* on someone is to sneakily listen to their conversation without them knowing. For example, *Marium told her brother to stop eavesdropping when she was talking to her friends on the phone.*

Did you know?

The lower edges of a roof are called the *eaves*. So, a person hanging around under the *eaves* and listening to other people's conversations would be described as an *eavesdropper*.

CORRESPOND

If you *correspond* with someone it means you are writing to them and they are writing back to you. Traditionally, people *corresponded* by letter, but nowadays you can *correspond* by email, text message and loads of other online messaging apps. When two people *correspond* with each other, they have a *correspondence*. A *correspondence* is also the word for the total collection of the messages the two people send between each other.

Other uses

When two things are closely linked to each other, you could say they *correspond*. For example, *The number of tickets sold corresponded with the number of people in the audience.* *Correspond* can also mean that two things match up or are in agreement. Journalists who report news on a particular subject are often called *correspondents*.

ATTENTIVE

An *attentive* person concentrates fully on whatever is being said or done. It's a similar word to 'attention'; if you are being *attentive*, you give your full attention. For example, *The teacher was surprised by how attentive his class was being.*

Other uses

Someone who puts a lot of effort into looking after another person could also be called *attentive*. For example, *When we visited Grandma in hospital, we saw that the nurses were being very attentive.*

MONOTONOUS

When something becomes boring because it is repeated over and over again, it is *monotonous*. A *monotonous* conversation is one that doesn't vary and keeps going over the same things. For example, *Eating spaghetti and meatballs every single day was becoming monotonous.*

Did you know?

Mono at the start of a word usually means 'one'. So, something that is *monotonous* has only one 'tone'. A very similar word is *monotone*, which can refer to a constant sound that doesn't vary or a picture that contains only one tone of colour. A black-and-white picture is 'monochrome'. Other uses

---

PRONOUNCE

The way you *pronounce* a word is the way you say it. Any two people might pronounce a word slightly differently, depending on their accents. Words are often *pronounced* differently to how they are spelled – which can sometimes make *pronunciation* tricky!

Spellcheck

Notice that, when writing the word *pronunciation*, *pronounce* loses its second o. That change also applies to the *pronunciation* of *pronunciation!* You *pronounce pronunciation* 'pro-nun-see-ae-shun'. Simple, right?

SINCERE

If you are being *sincere*, it means that you truly mean what you are saying or doing, and have no bad intentions. For example, *Marta sent her sincere apologies for not being able to come to the party.*

Just the opposite

The opposite of *sincere* is *insincere*. An *insincere* person is seen as false or untrustworthy, so it's not a nice thing to be called.

Spellcheck

Even though *sincere* is pronounced 'sin-seer', it has a c in the middle rather than an s.

Where does it come from?

Sincere comes from the Latin word sincērus, meaning 'clean or pure'. Someone who is being sincere has clean or pure intentions.

PREJUDICE

An unfair dislike or judgement of someone or something is called *prejudice*. A *prejudiced* opinion is not based on facts and can often be offensive to others. For example, if you decide you don't like someone because of the hat they are wearing, you are being *prejudiced* because the hat doesn't tell you anything about what the person is really like.

Spellcheck

Watch out for the *j* in the middle of *prejudice*. It's pronounced 'preh-joo-diss'. If you break the word down into smaller parts, its meaning and spelling make sense. *Pre* means 'before' and *judice* means 'judgement'. So, a *prejudiced* person is making a judgement before they know the facts.

PERSUADE

When you *persuade* someone, you are trying to convince them to do what you want them to do. Sales staff in shops are good at *persuading* people to buy something, and so are advertisements on TV. If you've ever wanted something just because you saw it in an advert, it probably means you have been *persuaded!*

Where does it come from?

Persuade comes from the Latin word persuādēre, where per means 'thoroughly' and suādēre means 'to urge or advise'.

SPEECH

When you talk, the words that come out of your mouth are *speech*. Sometimes, if people have problems with how they speak, they are helped by a *speech therapist*.

Other uses

If you *make a speech,* you stand up in front of an audience and say something you have prepared. If you have ever been to a wedding, you probably saw people making *speeches* there.

Spellcheck

The *aa* from 'speak' is replaced here with a second e. Remember it this way: sp**e**eches are **e**ntertaining.

RAPPORT

When you get along with someone really well, it's called having a *rapport*. A *rapport* is a close, friendly relationship.

Silence please

The *t* at the end of *rapport* is silent. It's pronounced 'rah-poar'.

NETWORK

The people you know can be called your *network*. You could have a *network* of friends or a *network* of family. When you set out to meet new people to add to your *network*, it's called *networking*.

Other uses

A *network* can be any group of things that are connected to each other. A *computer network*, for example, is a lot of computers that are all connected to the same system.

THIS ONE OR THAT ONE?

Words that sound alike, but are very different.

WEAR

It's not just clothes that you can *wear*. You can *wear* your hair up or *wear* a smile on your face. *Wear* means any act of putting something on yourself or adopting a style or look.

Other uses

If something *wears down,* it is being made smoother or weaker.

Not to be confused with...

Where (as in, *Where do you live?*).

BARE

Bare means uncovered. When a table is *bare*, it has nothing on top of it. When your body is *bare*, you're naked!

Not to be confused with...

Bear (a wild animal) or to *bear* (to carry something). If you really dislike something, you might say that you cannot *bear* it. On a particularly bad day you might say: *I cannot bear it when bears steal my clothes and leave me bare.*

BOAR

A *boar* can be either a male pig or a wild pig.

Not to be confused with...

Bore (to make someone feel *bored* by being uninteresting). *Bore* can also mean to make a deep, round hole in something. If a person's eyes *bore* into you, it means they are staring really hard at you, almost like they are *boring* a hole in the side of your head. It's not a nice feeling. Especially not when a *boar* does it.

HERD

A *herd* is a group of the same type of animal, all living or eating together. If you're very lucky, you might see a *herd* of elephants.

Not to be confused with...

Heard (to have listened to something). There's an easy way to remember the different spellings of these two: you use your **ear** to **hear**. Have you *heard* that one before?

> **Did you know?**
>
> *Herd* can also be used for people. If you're doing or thinking the same thing as lots of other people, it might be said that you're *following the herd*. And if you *herd* a crowd of people somewhere, you're making them move together in a group.

DEER

A *deer* is a wild animal that eats grass and leaves and has long legs to help it run fast. There are lots of different types of *deer*, such as elk, *reindeer* and *roe deer*. The males tend to be the ones with antlers, which are branch-like horns.

Not to be confused with...

Dear (a term of affection). This *dear* is normally used to show that someone or something is important to you. *My dear friend Jill baked this cake for me.* These days, you're probably unlikely to refer to people as *dear*, but you might still use it if writing a card, letter or email. *Dear Jill, thanks for baking me that cake!*

Anything else?

Dear can also be used to mean expensive (*That scarf is too dear*) or an expression of disappointment (*Oh dear*).

> ### Did you know?
> In most English-speaking countries, the plural of deer is *deer*. However, in some parts of the world you can also get away with using *deers*.

FUR

Fur is the thick, soft hair that covers the bodies of lots of animals. *Fur* and hair are exactly the same thing. Both are made from keratin (which is also in fingernails, hooves, feathers, horns and even wool).

Not to be confused with...

Fir (a tall evergreen tree with thin, needle-like leaves).

FOWL

Fowl is a very old word for birds. Nowadays, it's mainly used when talking about the type of birds used for meat or eggs, such as ducks, chickens, turkeys and geese.

Not to be confused with...

Foul (something dirty, smelly, unpleasant or offensive). In a sewer, you'd probably notice a *foul smell*. If you say a naughty word you might be accused of using *foul language*. In sport, you can also commit a *foul* – meaning that you've broken the rules.

Spellcheck

Remember, **owl** (as in, the bird) is in **fowl** (as in, the birds).

WHOSE

Use *whose* when talking about someone's belongings. For example, you might say, *She's the lady whose dog we look after.* Alternatively, you could use it in a question to find out who something belongs to, as in, *Whose car is this?*

Not to be confused with...

Who's (a shortened version of 'who is', with the apostrophe showing that a letter has been removed). For example, *Who's that man?*

FLEA

This tiny insect feeds on the blood of humans and animals. *Fleas* have no wings, so they jump around from one victim to the next, thirstily sucking their blood. Yuck!

In English, if you send someone away with a *flea in their ear,* it means that you've given them a sharp telling off. However, in some languages this expression means that you've been made suspicious by another person, and in other languages it means that you're fidgety. All of these sound better than having an actual *flea* in your ear!

Not to be confused with...

Flee (leave quickly or escape). Remember, when you *flee* you run away with sp**ee**d, while a *flea* simply l**ea**ps from place to place.

Did you know?

Flea circuses were a major attraction during the 19th and early 20th centuries. Despite their tiny size, *fleas* are incredibly good jumpers. The *flea* 'tamers' would attach the *fleas* to small pieces of circus equipment. Some *fleas* would even pull little chariots. However, warmer, cleaner homes and the arrival of the vacuum cleaner made *fleas* much less common, and the *flea circus* became a thing of the past.

COMPLIMENT

We all love receiving one of these. A *compliment* is a really nice thing that someone says about you or something you've done.

Not to be confused with...

Complement (when two things go well together). For example, if your shoes really *complement* your hat, it doesn't mean they're saying nice things about your headwear. It means your shoes and hat look good together. Try remembering the difference between *complement* and *compliment* this way: **I** *love a compliment.*

HEEL

The bit at the back of your foot below your ankle is your *heel*. Socks and shoes have heels too. Some shoes even have *high heels*. Some people also call the end slice of a bread loaf the *heel*.

Not to be confused with...

Heal (when something that has been injured or broken gets better again) or *he'll* (short for 'he will'). Did you know?

Did you know?

An *Achilles heel* is a person's weak spot (for example, *His Achilles heel is his laziness*). This comes from the Greek myth of Achilles, who was dipped into the magical River Styx by his mother when he was a baby, to make

> his body strong. Because he was held by his *heel*, it wasn't touched by the water, so remained weak.

CHILLI

A *chilli* is a hot-tasting pepper. Despite being small, it can pack a real punch when you add it to your food.

Other uses

The popular meal *chilli con carne* is often shortened to just *chilli*. *Con carne* translates from Spanish into English as 'with meat'.

Spellcheck

You might have seen this word written as either *chilli* or *chili*. That's because it is spelled with two *l*'s in the UK but just one in the US.

Not to be confused with...

Chilly (meaning cold) or *Chile* (a country in South America).

> ### Did you know?
> *Chilli* spiciness can be so extreme that it even has its own measurement system, called the Scoville scale. The world's hottest *chilli*, the Carolina reaper, measures over 1.6 million Scoville heat units (SHUs). By comparison, the average *jalapeño chilli*, that you might have tried at home, measures just 5,000.

YOUR

Your is used when something belongs or relates to someone. For example, *Please ask your dog to stop peeing on my leg.*

Not to be confused with...

You're (a shortened version of 'you' and 'are', with the apostrophe showing that a letter is missing). For example, *You're a great friend, but I wish your dog would stop peeing on my leg.*

THERE

This might seem like one of the simplest words around, but it's a really easy one to get caught out on. You use *there* to refer to a place or position, but also to say that something exists. So, you could say *The cakes are over there* to explain where the cakes are. Or you could say *There is a type of dog called a Labrador* to state that Labradors are a thing that exists.

Not to be confused with...

Their (belonging to them, as in, *Their clothes are very wet*) or *they're* (shortened version of 'they' and 'are', as in, *They're very nice people*).

They're there v there there

One is a thing you might say to a baby when it's crying. The other is something you'd say when pointing out where your friends are. But can you work out which one's which? The answer is at the bottom of the opposite page.

'There there' is for the crying baby. 'They're there' means 'they are over there'.

AISLE

An *aisle* (pronounced the same way as 'I'll') is a gap or passageway, often between rows of chairs or shelves. In supermarkets, the rows you walk down are called *aisles*. You might also have heard people asking for an *aisle seat* on a flight or at the theatre. Those seats tend to be handy if you want extra leg room or plan on making an early exit (not that an early exit from a plane is advisable).

Not to be confused with...

Isle (an island) or *I'll* (shortened version of 'I will').

Silence please

The s in *aisle* is silent. It's actually pretty unusual for an English word to have a silent s. Can you think of any other examples? There are a few at the bottom of page.

ADVICE

At some point or another you've probably given or received some *advice*. This is when a person tells someone else what they think they should do. An example of good advice is: *Always look both ways before crossing the road.* An example of bad advice is: *Jump off that cliff!*

Not to be confused with...

Advise (if you advise someone to do something, you are giving them *advice*, as in, *I would advise you to wear a helmet when cycling*).

COLONEL

A *colonel* is a senior military officer, normally either in the army, US air force or marines. Despite the spelling, it's pronounced 'kuhr-nuhl'.

Not to be confused with...

Kernel (the part inside the shell of a seed or nut that you can eat).

Did you know?

> The word *colonel* has changed a lot over time. The Italian word *colonnello* was changed by the French to *coronel*. The English then started using a combination of the two, spelling it with an *l* but pronouncing it with an *r* – and it's stayed that way ever since.

GENES

You look the way you do because of your *genes*. A *gene* is the part of a cell that determines things such as hair and eye colour. All living things have *genes* that have been passed on to them from their parents.

Not to be confused with...

Jeans (trousers made from denim).
English words with a silent *s*: Arkansas, debris, island, isle, viscount

REIGN

When kings or queens *reign*, it means they are the rulers of their countries. They sit on the throne, govern and hold power. If that king or queen is especially nasty, their time in charge might be described as a *reign of terror*. But it's not just royalty who can *reign*. A person who is really successful in a particular area might also be said to *reign*. For example, a sports star who dominates their sport might become the *reigning world champion*.

Other uses

Reign is not just used for people. Silence can *reign* over a place (if it's really quiet) and confusion can *reign* over a situation (if it's really chaotic).

Not to be confused with...

Rein (a leather strap on a horse) or *rain* (water falling from the sky).

MEDAL

A *medal* is the metal disc you might get given as an award for coming first, second or third in a sporting event. *Medals* are also sometimes awarded to people for doing something brave.

Not to be confused with...

Meddle (to interfere with or change something, when you haven't been asked to).

DESERT

A *desert* is a place where there's not much water. It's often extremely hot and very few plants can survive.

Other uses

If you *desert* a place or person, it means you have abandoned them. When everyone abandons a place so that there's no one left, it could be described *as deserted*.

Did you know?

There are also polar deserts at the North and South Pole. Even though these places are very cold, they are considered *deserts* because they hardly ever experience rainfall.

Not to be confused with...

Dessert. That one extra little s makes a very big difference here. A *dessert* is a sweet treat or pudding, usually eaten at the end of a meal. Struggling to remember which one's which? Try thinking about it this way: *de**ss**ert* has an extra s for added sweetne**ss.**

PRINCIPAL

A *principal* can be another name for a head teacher at a school or college. It can also be used to describe an issue that is of the highest importance. For example, *The principal purpose of this book is to explain the meanings of 365 words.*

Not to be confused with...

Principle (a moral rule or strong belief, for example, *Daria refused to cheat on the exam because it was against her principles*). Struggling to remember the difference? Think of principal being the one with *pal* at the end. A *princi**pal*** is a person, and so is your **pal!**

PIECE

A *piece* is a part of something that has been taken off or separated from the rest. For example, a *piece* of chocolate is a square of chocolate that has been broken off a bar. A *piece* of clothing is one item of clothing from a selection. A *piece* can also mean 'some'. For example, if you give someone a *piece* of paper then you are giving them 'some' paper.

Easy peasy

A *piece of cake* can mean a slice of cake, but it can also mean that something is easy to do. If you say your homework is a *piece of cake*, you mean it's simple and not worth worrying about (unless, of course, your homework was from cooking class and you actually did have to make some cake).

Not to be confused with...

Peace (a time of no war or conflict). You've probably heard the term *peace and quiet,* meaning 'calm'. The phrase *hold your peace* means you should say nothing, even if you really want to give your opinion.

> **Did you know?**
>
> In Scotland, *piece* is a slang term for a sandwich, and a *piece box* is a lunch box.

STATIONERY

Stationery covers lots of different materials and equipment you would use for writing, including paper, pens, pencils, rulers, folders, envelopes, staplers and all of that other good stuff that you probably have to use when doing your homework. Ugh.

Not to be confused with...

Stationary (staying still and not moving from one spot). How can you remember which ending you need? Well, e is for 'envelope', and there's an **e** in stationery.

WEATHER

Weather is the condition of the atmosphere in a certain place at a certain time. It could be hot or cold, raining or dry, windy or calm, and loads of other things in between. Rocks and other materials can be *weathered* by the *weather*, too. This means that they've been exposed to so much *weather* over time that they've changed their appearance.

Not to be confused with...

Whether (used to introduce a choice between two possibilities). For example, *Luis wasn't sure whether he wanted to stay at the party or go home.*

Did you know?
If you're *weathering a storm*, it could literally mean you're all wrapped up and managing to stay dry – but it more likely means that you're coping well in a crisis.

PROFIT

A *profit* is a benefit or advantage. If you *make a profit*, you make money! If you sell something for more than it cost you, the extra money that you earn is your *profit*. Be careful, though: if you earn less than you have spent, then you'll make a loss instead.

Not to be confused with...

Prophet (a person believed to have the ability to pass on a message from God). A *prophet* can also be someone who predicts the future.

EFFECT

Ever cried at a sad story or laughed at a funny movie? If so, those things were having an *effect* on you. An effect is the change caused by one thing to another. In these examples, the changes were your tears or laughter.

Other uses

Effect can also refer to a person's belongings. If you are admitted to hospital, for example, the items you have with you at the time might be referred to as your *personal effects*.

Not to be confused with...

Affect (to influence or change). If something or someone affects you, they make you feel a certain way. Most of the time, something *affects* something else to produce an *effect*. Try remembering the difference this way: **effect** is an **end** result, while **affect** is an **action**.

BOO!

Words to make you turn all the lights on.

HALLOWEEN

The evening before All Hallows' Day is All Hallows' Eve, which you're more likely to know as *Halloween*. It falls on the last day of October, and lots of people celebrate it by dressing up in costumes, carving pumpkins and going trick-or-treating.

H is for horror

Remember that *Halloween* needs a capital *H* at the beginning because it is a proper noun (meaning it's the name of a specific event, place or person). All the better to haunt you with!

Did you know?

Traditionally it was believed that *Halloween* was the night of the year when people were most likely to see ghosts, witches and other terrifying things that go bump in the night.

CAULDRON

A *cauldron* is a big pot used for cooking delicious stews over a fire – so what's so spooky about that? Well, it's also what witches are said to use when they're up to no good. No classic fairy tale is complete without a wicked witch casting an evil spell over a bubbling *cauldron*.

Other uses

A bad situation can be referred to as a *cauldron*, too. For example, you could say, *Eve's mind was a bubbling cauldron of anger.*

PETRIFY

Get ready to be afraid. Very afraid! If something is *petrifying*, it is not just scary, but so scary you may not be able to even move. *He* was frozen with fear. The haunted house petrified him.

Other uses

If you *petrify* something, you change it into a fossilized form. You probably already know about fossils, which are dead plants or animals that have turned to stone over millions of years. Those plants and animals have been *petrified*.

CEMETERY

A *cemetery* is a place where dead people's bodies are buried. It is another word for a graveyard. *Cemetery* comes from the Greek word koimētērion, meaning 'room for sleeping', and that comes from *koiman*, which means 'to put to sleep'. Chilling!

Spelling trick (or treat)

Cemetery has three e's in it, so you could think of someone screaming *EEE!* as they walk past the scary *cemetery*.

TOMB

A *tomb* is a large grave, either above or below the ground. Many *tombs* are built as a monument to a specific person who has died, but the word can also be used for any burial place. For example, if sailors die at sea, you might say, *The ocean bed was their tomb.*

Silence please

The *b* is silent — just like (hopefully) the *tomb's* residents. It's pronounced 'toom'. Other words ending with a silent *b* include bomb, climb, comb, numb and thumb.

Grave situation

Some other words you might hear for gravesites include:
- mausoleum (a building that houses graves of wealthy people)
- crypt (a burial room underneath a church or cathedral)
- catacomb (underground tunnels used for burying the dead).

COFFIN

There are some boxes you want to open and some you definitely do not. A *coffin* is the second kind of box because what's usually inside is a dead body (or perhaps, occasionally, a sleeping vampire).

Not to be confused with...

Coughing (a way of clearing your throat, pronounced 'coff-ing').

Did you know?
A horse's foot has a bone in it called the *coffin* bone.

EERIE

Mwah ha ha! What's that *eerie* cackling sound? When you call something *eerie*, you mean that it is odd, scary or frightening. It probably makes you feel a bit nervous, too. You might describe a place as *eerily quiet* or *eerily empty*, which suggests that, not only is it quiet or empty, but it's a little bit spooky, too.

Not to be confused with...

Eyrie (a castle, or bird's nest, that has been built somewhere high up, such as on a clifftop or mountaintop).

SPECTRE

A *spectre* is one of many names for a ghost. Some of the others include ghoul, spirit, phantom, apparition and poltergeist. Despite the misleading spelling, it's prounounced 'speck-tur'.

SUPERNATURAL

If something is *supernatural*, it is impossible to explain using the laws of science. Some people believe in *supernatural* creatures, such as ghosts, but their existence has never been proven.

WARLOCK

As much as it sounds like it, this isn't some sort of funny contraption to bolt on to your door. A *warlock* is actually a man who practises black magic or witchcraft.

MACABRE

Something that is *macabre* is very frightening or unpleasant, and most probably involves a nasty injury or death. A *macabre* film or book is one that has a dark, gruesome story.

Spellcheck

You've probably already noticed that *macabre* has an odd spelling. This is because of its French origins. It's pronounced 'mack-ab-rah'.

BORROWED LANGUAGE

Words that are English ... or are they?

PAPARAZZI

Paparazzi are photographers who take pictures of famous people. This snappy word is the plural of the Italian word *paparazzo*. The word sometimes has negative undertones because some *paparazzi* invade celebrities' private lives to get their photographs.

Where does it come from?

Paparazzo was the name of a photographer character in an Italian movie from 1960 called *La Dolce Vita*. He was actually based on a real person.

Other words taken from Italian

- al dente (food that is cooked not too hard or too soft)
- alfresco (outdoors)
- espresso (a strong coffee)
- pepperoni (in Italy, *peperone* is the word for a bell pepper, but in English it changes to 'pepperoni' and is a spicy sausage)

PIÑATA

Get ready for a birthday bash! A *piñata* (that accent above the *n* means the word is pronounced 'pin-yah-tah') is a paper or clay shape decorated in bright colours and stuffed with treats. At parties, children wear blindfolds and take turns to hit the piñata with a stick until it breaks open and the treats are released. *Piñata* is a Spanish word, but it's thought that the game came from China.

Other words taken from Spanish

- patio (a flat concrete outdoor area where people can relax)
- siesta (a nap taken in the early afternoon)

KINDERGARTEN

A *kindergarten* is a type of school for very young children, where they learn by playing. It's originally a German word, with *kinder* meaning 'children' and *garten* meaning 'garden'. So it literally translates as 'children's garden'.

Surprise!

If you've ever had a Kinder Surprise chocolate egg, now you know what the name means. Kinder Surprise eggs have been banned from the United States for over 40 years because of fears that kids might choke on the tiny toys hidden inside.

Other words taken from German

- delicatessen (a shop that sells cold meats and cheeses)
- rucksack (a bag you carry on your back, like a backpack)

ENTREPRENEUR

An *entrepreneur* is someone who comes up with lots of new and original business ideas, and is able to make money out of them. *Entrepreneur* is a French word, but we use it in English, too.

Other words taken from French

- ballet (a dance that tells a story without talking or singing)
- café (a place where you can buy drinks and food)
- croissant (a sweet pastry rolled into a crescent shape)

GUNG-HO

Gung-ho means to be excited or to rush into a situation without proper thought. However, *gung-ho* originally comes from the Mandarin

Chinese word gōnghé, which translates into English as 'work together'.

Other words taken from Chinese

- kung fu (a Chinese form of self-defence)
- dim sum (dumplings stuffed with meat or other fillings)
- wok (a type of frying pan)

SCHMOOZE

If you *schmooze*, you talk to someone in a friendly way. It comes from *schmues*, which means 'chat' in Yiddish.[3]

Other words taken from Yiddish

- klutz (a clumsy person)
- kosher (can either mean authentic, or allowed by religious laws)
- schlep (an inconvenient journey)

COOKIE

A *cookie* is a sweet treat that can be either crunchy or chewy. It comes from the Dutch word *koekje* or *koek*, meaning 'cake'.

---

[3] Yiddish itself derives from German, Hebrew and a few other languages. Traditionally, it has mainly been used by Jewish people in Europe.

Cookie or biscuit?

In the UK, a *cookie* and a biscuit are more or less the same thing. However, in North America, a biscuit is a savoury bread, often served with gravy.

Not to be confused with...

Kooky (a way of describing someone who is fun and unusual).

Did you know?

When you go online, small files get saved on to your computer so that the websites you've visited can remember who you are. These files are also called *cookies*. Some people think that might be because Hansel and Gretel dropped *cookie* crumbs to remember where they'd been.

Other words taken from Dutch

- bluff (to deceive or mislead)
- spook (a ghost)

TREK

Trek means a long, slow journey, often on foot (but not always). If someone describes their journey to meet you as a *bit of trek,* it means it took them a long time and probably wasn't very much fun. *Trek* is Afrikaans[4] in origin, hence the unusual spelling (you'd probably expect it to be 'treck').

Other words taken from Afrikaans

- aardvark (a burrowing mammal with a long tongue and snout)
- meerkat (a small African mongoose).

---

[4] Afrikaans evolved from Dutch. It is an official language of South Africa.

SAFARI

A *safari* is a trip to look for animals (often African animals, such as lions and rhinos) in their natural habitat. The word originates from the Arabic *safara*, meaning 'to travel'.

Other words taken from Arabic

- coffee (a hot drink)
- lemon (a sour yellow fruit)

GURU

A *guru* is a Hindu or Sikh religious teacher or leader who gives spiritual guidance. Nowadays, the word is also used more widely for anyone who is an expert on a particular subject. For example, a person who knows a lot about cooking might get called a *food guru*. Guru originally comes from the Sanskrit[5] word *guruh*, meaning 'weighty'.

Other words taken from Sanskrit

- avatar (an image that represents someone)
- chit (a short official note such as a receipt)

YULE

People tend to think *Yule* is just another word for Christmas, but it actually came before the Christian festival of Christmas had even been thought of. *Yule* derives from the Viking word *jól*, a pagan[6] festival celebrating the winter solstice[7]

---

[5] Sanskrit is an ancient language of India, with a history dating back thousands of years.

[6] Pagans are people whose religious beliefs are much older than Christianity and the other main religions.

[7] The winter solstice is the shortest day of the year.

Other words taken from the Vikings

- blunder (a silly mistake)
- ransack (when you search for something, making a place untidy)

KARAOKE

Originating from Japan, *karaoke* is a type of entertainment where wannabe singers choose their favourite songs, then sing along to them. A *karaoke machine* plays the music and also helps you out by showing you the words and when to sing them. If you love pretending to be a pop star or like a singalong, then *karaoke* is the thing for you!

Other words taken from Japanese

- kawaii (an artistic style that is bright, bold, colourful and cute)

- origami (the art of folding paper into different shapes and models)

> **Did you know?**
>
> Usually in English we don't pronounce the e at the end of words, but we do with this one. It's pronounced 'kah-ree-oh-kee'.

AMBIGUOUS

If something is *ambiguous*, it means that it is unclear or confusing. Here's an example of an *ambiguous* statement: *Kate bathed her cat wearing a funny hat.* Is Kate wearing the hat or is the cat? You can't tell, which makes it *ambiguous*. This word originates from the Latin *ambiguus*, meaning 'doubtful or changeable'.

Other words taken from Latin

- futile (pointless)
- plausible (believable)

ANONYMOUS

If a person is *anonymous*, it means their name isn't known. It comes from the Greek word *anōnumos*, where an means 'without' and onoma means 'name'. Sometimes, people wish to remain *anonymous*. For example, *The money was donated to the charity by a famous celebrity who would like to remain anonymous.*

Other uses

Sometimes, *anonymous* is used to describe something that is a bit dull and featureless. For example, *A town full of anonymous buildings that all look the same.*

Other words taken from Greek

- metropolis (a big and busy city)
- phobia (an irrational fear or hatred of something)

YOUR HISTORY

Words about past times (not pastimes).

PREHISTORIC

Some things are so old that they existed before anyone could write about them. Those things are *prehistoric*. You've probably heard this word used a lot in relation to dinosaurs and cave people. Although there are no written records of *prehistoric* times, we can still learn about them thanks to discoveries of things like cave paintings, fossils and ancient tools.

Break it down

Pre means 'before', so *prehistory* literally means 'before history'.

ANCIENT

If something is *ancient*, it is extremely old and from the very distant past. It is used particularly for anything that comes from before the end of the Roman Empire (which was over 1,500 years ago). Civilizations from a very long time ago are often called ancient – particularly *ancient Rome, ancient Greece and ancient Egypt*.

Spellcheck

This word breaks the '*i* before *e*, except after *c*' rule. That's because it derives from the French word ancien. Ancient is pronounced 'ayn-shunt'.

ARCHAEOLOGY

Archaeology is the study of human cultures using the remains of people's belongings. Those remains could be as big as the buildings they lived in, or as small as the tools they used, or even tiny pieces of the clothing or jewellery they wore. A person who studies *archaeology is called an archaeologist.*

Archaeologist v paleontologist

A lot of people think *archaeologists* study dinosaurs, but they don't. *Archaeologists* are only interested in humans. The people who study life from before humans came along – including dinosaurs – are called *paleontologists*.

Spellcheck

Don't let the *ch* in the middle of *archaeology* trip you up. It's actually pronounced 'ark-ee-oh-low-jee'.

ARTEFACT

A historic object made by humans is called an *artefact*. *Artefacts* are important and interesting discoveries as they can tell us a lot about the past. If you look around any museum, you're likely to see lots of amazing *artefacts*.

Where does it come from?

Artefact comes from Latin, where *arte* means 'by or using art', and *factum* means 'something made'.

MEDIEVAL

Medieval refers to anything from the period of time known as the Middle Ages, which came between the 5th and 14th centuries. You might say, for example, We *went on a trip to see a medieval castle.*

Spellcheck

Note that, despite the end part sounding a little like 'evil', there's an *a* there rather than an *i*.

VOYAGE

A long journey by ship or spacecraft, especially one that sets out to discover new places, is called a *voyage*.

Spellcheck

Voyage is pronounced 'voy-idj'. Although the last part doesn't sound like 'age' when you say it, you could remember how to spell it by thinking: long vo**yages** ages take **ages.**

CONQUER

Conquer means to take control of a place by defeating its people. A *conquer or* is someone who *conquers* a country or area of land.

Did you know?

William I, who was King of England from 1066 until 1087, was so good at *conquering* that he became known as 'William the *Conqueror'*. He was from Normandy (part of modern-day France), but became England's king

> by conquering it, in what is known as the Norman *Conquest.*

Other uses

If you overcome something difficult, you could say you have conquered it. You might *conquer* a fear of heights by bungee jumping, for example.

Not to be confused with...

Conker (another word for a horse chestnut).

EMPIRE

When one country controls any number of other countries, those countries become part of an *empire*. Throughout history, rulers have often built *empires* by sending their armies to invade and conquer other places. One of the most famous *empires* in history was the *Roman Empire,* which saw many parts of Europe, Asia and northern Africa taken over and governed by *Roman emperors*.

Other uses

Any country that calls its leader an *emperor* can also be called an *empire*. In business, very large and powerful companies are also sometimes described as *empires*.

DYNASTY

When several generations of a family rule a country for many years, it's called a *dynasty* (pronounced 'dih-nah-stee'). There have been lots of famous dynasties in history. One well-known example is the *Ming Dynasty*, which saw members of the Zhu family rule as emperors of China for 276 years, from 1368 until 1644.

PHARAOH

In ancient Egypt, the country's ruler was called the *Pharaoh*. Egypt's people believed that the *pharaohs* were a direct link to the Gods, and they built the pyramids to be used as the *pharaohs'* tombs.

Spellcheck

Pharaoh is not only a tough word to spell, but also to say. It's pronounced 'fare-oe'.

SUFFRAGE

Suffrage means the right to vote in elections. In a democracy there is universal *suffrage*, which means that all adults (with a few small exceptions) are allowed to vote. In some countries, people are still fighting for *suffrage* even today.

Where does it come from?

This strange-sounding word comes from the Latin suffrāgium, which means 'a vote'. Note that it has nothing at all to do with suffering!

Other uses

If you're especially eagle-eyed, you might see the word *suffrage* in old chapels and churches.

That's because *suffrage* can also be used to mean 'prayer'.

> ### Did you know?
> In the early 20th century, women in many countries did not have the right to vote. The women who campaigned for that to change in the UK and USA became known as *suffragettes*. Today, men and women have equal voting rights in both countries.

ARCHITECTURE

The style in which a building has been designed and built is its *architecture*. This can be very helpful to historians, as the design of a building can help them to work out when it was built. In the UK, styles of *architecture* are often named after the king or queen of the time. For example, Victorian buildings were built in the time of Queen Victoria, and Elizabethan buildings are from the time of Queen Elizabeth I.

Did you know?

A person who designs and plans new buildings is called an *architect*.

PORTCULLIS

Old castles often had a heavy metal gate that could be raised to let people in or lowered to keep enemies out! This style of gate is called a *portcullis*.

Where does it come from?

Porte is French for 'door'. The *cullis* part comes from the Latin cōlāre which means 'to filter'.

MUSIC TIME

Words for those song-and-dance moments.

RHYTHM

A regular, repeated pattern of beats is known as a *rhythm*. For example, *Mohammed tapped his feet to the rhythm of the music.*

Spellcheck

This is one of the toughest words to spell, but remembering this phrase should help: **r**hythm **h**elps **y**our **t**wisting **h**ips **m**ove.

Did you know?

Rhythm is the joint-longest English word that does not contain any of the vowels *a, e, i, o* or *u*. Others that are the same length include spryly and Sphynx.

RHYME

If two words *rhyme*, it means they have a similar sound. *Rhyming* words are often used at the ends of lines in songs and poems.

Rhyme time

Despite its odd spelling, *rhyme* is pronounced 'rime'. Or, to explain it another way, it *rhymes* with crime, prime, dime and slime.

Other uses

A *rhyme* can also be a short poem or song that contains *rhyming* words (a *nursery rhyme*, for example).

LYRICS

The words of a song are called *lyrics*. If you have a favourite song, you probably know its *lyrics* off by heart.

Other uses

If something is described as *lyrical*, it means it is romantic or poetic (or both!). If someone is said to be waxing *lyrical*, it means they are talking with lots of enthusiasm. For example, *Dominic was waxing lyrical about his video-game collection.*

SCORE

Music that is composed for a movie, TV show or play is called a *score*.

Other uses

Outside music, a score is the number of points or goals someone has in a game. For example, *Did you see the game? What was the score?* You can also *score* a goal and get a *score* in a test. And you can *score* a surface with something sharp, meaning that you cut into it.

> ### Did you know?
>
> *Score* also means 'approximately 20'. So if a score of piranhas is heading towards you, you'd better get out of the way!

VERSE

A group of lines that come together to form part of a song or poem is called a verse. The lines tend to have rhythm and often rhyme at the end, but they don't have to.

Not to be confused with...

Versus (when someone competes against someone else, as in, *It was Manchester United versus Barcelona in the soccer match. Versus* is often shortened to just *v, v.* or *vs*).

CHORUS

The part of a song that is repeated throughout the song is called the chorus. It often comes between the verses. For example, *Nadia didn't know the lyrics to the verses of the song, but she did sing along with the chorus.*

Other uses

Chorus is sometimes used as another word for a choir (pronounced 'kwy-uhr'), which is a group of people who sing together. Outside music, a *chorus* can be any group of people saying the same thing. For example, *There was a chorus of complaints about the TV show.* There's also the *dawn chorus,* which is the name given to the loud chirping sounds made by birds first thing in the morning.

SOLO

Solo means 'on your own'. So, in music, when a person sings or plays an instrument on their own, it's called a *solo performance. Solo* is pronounced 'so-low', but has nothing to do with being 'low'.

Where does it come from?

Solo comes from the Latin *solus,* meaning 'alone'.

BALLAD

A slow, romantic song is called a *ballad*. You can probably think of a few *ballads*, as there tend to be lots of them in the music charts. A *ballad* can also be a long story or poem.

MELODY

When you find a song catchy, it's probably because it has a good *melody*. The *melody* is the tune, and it's the part that can often get stuck in your head.

PITCH

Pitch is how high or low a musical note sounds. Someone who can sing or recognize musical notes correctly is said to have *perfect pitch*.

Other uses

Pitch is one of those words that has loads of uses. Here are a few of them:
- a field that sports matches are played on
- a powerful throw, especially in baseball
- a presentation where someone puts forward an idea
- to fall forward
- to put up a tent

- the sudden movement of a boat up and down on the waves
- a way of describing complete darkness (as in, pitch-black).

CHORD

When musical notes are tunefully played or sung together at the same time, they form a *chord*.

Not to be confused with...

Cord (a piece of string or thin rope made from twisted strands).

Did you know?

If something *strikes a chord* with you, it means that it got you feeling all emotional. *Debbie's moving speech struck a chord with everyone in the audience.*

BASS

The lowest and deepest sounds in music are called *bass* sounds (pronounced 'base'). You can have *bass* instruments or even a *bass* voice. A person who plays *bass guitar* is called a *bassist*. On radios and sound systems, the *bass* button or dial lets you turn the volume of the lowest notes up or down.

Other uses

Bass is also a type of fish. However, the fish is pronounced 'bahss'.

Not to be confused with...

Base (the bottom of something, or a place where you spend most of your time).

COMPOSER

A *composer* is someone who writes music. The word is often associated with famous classical *composers,* such as Beethoven and Mozart, but anyone who *composes* music is a *composer.*

Where does it come from?

Composer comes from the Latin word *componere,* meaning 'put together'. It makes sense, when you think about it, as musical pieces need to be 'put together' by *composers.*

CONDUCTOR

Have you ever noticed the person who stands in front of a choir or orchestra and waves their arms around? Well, that person is a *conductor.* The *conductor* uses arm gestures to let everyone know what they should be doing. They tell people when to start singing or playing their part and how loud or soft they should be, and also help them to keep in time. It's a very important (and difficult!) job.

Other uses

You get *conductors* outside of music, too. A *conductor* is the person on a bus or train who checks passengers' tickets. In science, a *conductor* is any substance that heat or electricity can pass through.

ENSEMBLE

When a group of musicians play or sing together, they are called an *ensemble* (pronounced 'ohn-sohm-buhl'). For example, *Louie and his best friend were part of a string ensemble at school*. This means that Louie and his friend play musical instruments with strings together, but the instruments could be different.

Ensemble v orchestra

Both of these words refer to a group of musicians, but an orchestra is a specific kind of *ensemble* that includes people playing a wide range of different instruments.

Other uses

You can also have *ensembles* of actors or dancers. If a movie is said to have an *ensemble cast*, it means there are a large number of key actors, rather than just one or two in lead roles.

SYMPHONY

A long piece of music written for orchestras to perform is called a *symphony*. A *symphony* usually has four sections, which are called movements.

Other uses

Because a *symphony* involves lots of instruments coming together in harmony (at the same time), the word *symphony* has also come to mean any situation where things work well together. So, for example, a great painting might contain a *symphony* of colours.

PERCUSSION

Musical instruments that you play by shaking or hitting them with your hand or a beater are called *percussion* instruments. These instruments include cymbals, drums and even the little triangle you might have played in music class at school. Someone who plays this kind of instrument is a *percussionist*.

Where does it come from?

Percussion comes from the Latin word *percutere*, which means 'to strike forcibly'. If you've ever seen a *percussionist* play, that translation will make a lot of sense!

Did you know?

Percussion is also one of the four sections that normally make up an orchestra. The other three sections are:
• strings (instruments like violins and cellos)
• woodwind (instruments like flutes and oboes)
• brass (instruments like horns and trumpets).
Some orchestras also have a keyboard section.

TAMBOURINE

A *tambourine* is a circular musical instrument with round metal pieces around the edge. When you tap or shake the *tambourine*, the metal pieces jangle together and make a very pleasing sound.

Spellcheck

You may have had a go at playing a *tambourine*, but have you ever had a go at spelling it? Try breaking it down into smaller chunks, 'tam-bour-ine', and tapping your leg as if you were tapping a *tambourine* to the three beats as you say the sounds.

CYMBAL

A *cymbal* is a flat, round musical instrument, usually made of brass. It is either hit with a stick or with another *cymbal*. You may have heard two *cymbals* clanging together and making a very loud sound. As you might expect, *cymbals* are lots of fun to play.

Spellcheck

Cymbal has an unusual *cym* at the start, which is actually pronounced 'sim'.

Not to be confused with...

Symbol (a mark or sign that represents something) or *sambal* (a spicy relish from Southeast Asia).

HYMN

A religious song that praises God is called a *hymn*. You're most likely to hear *hymns* sung inside a church.

Spellcheck

If you think the spelling of *hymn* looks unusual, it's probably because it contains none of the vowels *a*, *e*, *i*, *o* or *u*, and it also has a silent n. Despite the very tricky spelling, it's pronounced 'him'. It may help you to remember the first letters of the phrase **have you made noise**.

Not to be confused with...

Him (the word used to refer to a male person or animal, for example, *I want to help him*).

WORDS OF ART

Words for when you're feeling creative.

SKETCH

A drawing that is done quickly is called a *sketch*. An artist will often do a *sketch* to practise before working on a more detailed picture. *Sketches* tend to be quite simple, without much detail or colour.

Other uses

A *comedy sketch* is a short, funny performance acted out by comedians. You might see a whole *sketch show*, where lots of sketches are performed one after the other.

> ### Did you know?
> In some places, *sketchy* is a slang word used to describe someone who is unreliable or who can't be trusted.

SCULPT

To *sculpt* is to carve or shape something out of a material. Objects can be *sculpted* from clay, wood, stone and loads of other substances. The end result is a piece of art called a *sculpture*.

Other uses

Sculpt isn't just used in art. Everything from the shape of the land around you to your own hair and body can be *sculpted*.

PORTRAIT

A drawing, painting or photograph of a person is called a *portrait*. If you create a portrait of yourself, it's called a *self-portrait*. You might even say that *self-portraits* were the original selfies!

Other uses

Today, the word *portrait* is commonly used to describe a sheet of paper or a screen that is held so that it's taller than it is wide.

LANDSCAPE

The *landscape* is everything you see when you look around. *Landscape* art is a drawing or painting of that view.

Other uses

If you *landscape* an area of land, you change it to make it look better. A sheet of paper or a screen held so that it's wider than it is tall is also referred to as *landscape*.

TONE

In art, tone is the lightness or darkness of shading in a picture. For example, light green and dark green are different *tones* of green.

Other uses

Tone is also used for lots of other things outside art. Have you ever heard someone say *I don't like your tone?* They're saying that the way you are speaking is giving them a bad feeling. *Tone* can also describe the quality of a sound, or the atmosphere of a place. You can even *tone* your body, which means that you make yourself physically stronger by doing lots of exercise.

OBSERVE

To *observe* something is to do more than just look at it. When you observe something, you are looking at it very closely to try to understand more about it. That is what artists need to do when they draw things.

Other uses

If you *observe* a law, custom, or tradition, it means that you follow or obey it. For example, *The crowd observed a minute's silence in memory of those lost in the war.*

COLLAGE

If you arrange different bits of paper or other materials together to make a picture, it's called a *collage*.

Where does it come from?

Collage comes from the French word *coller*, meaning 'paste'.

Not to be confused with...

College (a type of school, usually for older students). One way of learning the difference between *collage* and *college* is to remember that **a** is for **a**rt and **e** is for **e**ducation.

MEDIUM

Any substance used to create art, such as paint or ink, is called a *medium*. For example, *The famous artist Vincent van Gogh often used the medium of oil paint.* These substances are often referred to together as *media*, which is the plural of *medium*.

Other uses

Outside art, a form of communication might be described as a *medium*. TV is a *medium*, and so is radio and the internet (you've probably heard these being referred to as the *media*). A *medium* can also be a person who claims to be able to talk to the spirits of dead people.

In the middle

Something that is neither large nor small, but somewhere in between, is *medium* in size. For example, *Maria ordered a medium milkshake.*

Where does it come from?

Medium originally comes from the Latin word *medius*, which means 'middle'.

BOOK TALK

Words you might see in your local library or bookshop.

DICTIONARY

A book or online resource that lists words in alphabetical order and tells you their meanings is called a *dictionary*. If you ever hear a person use the phrase *They must have swallowed a dictionary*, it's a jokey way of saying that someone is using lots of big, complicated words.

Where does it come from?

Dictionary comes from the Latin word dictionarium, meaning 'collection of words'. It's similar to diction, dictate and dictator, which also relate to words and how they are used. These words are all connected by the Latin word dīcere, meaning 'to speak'.

THESAURUS

Instead of listing words and their meanings like a dictionary, a *thesaurus* provides 'synonyms' for each word. Synonyms are alternative words that have a similar meaning (e.g. 'huge' is a synonym for 'large'). A *thesaurus* can come in really handy when you're writing and don't want to use the same word twice.

Did you know?

Saurus means 'treasury' in Greek. A treasury is a book containing a collection of valuable content, or 'treasures'. Lots of dinosaurs have names ending in *saurus*, but that comes from a different Greek word – *sauros*, meaning 'lizard'.

ENCYCLOPEDIA

A reference source that contains lots of facts about many things is called an *encyclopedia*. Because there is so much information to be squeezed into them, *encyclopedias* are often split into large sets of separate books (also known as volumes).

Spellcheck

Encyclopedia is a tricky word to spell, but it's not so bad if you break it into bite-sized chunks and remember that the part in the middle is spelled the same way as the beginning of 'cycle'. It's pronounced 'en-sye-kloe-pee-dee-ah.'

Did you know?

Encyclopedia is one of those annoying words that actually has more than one correct spelling. You can also stick an *a* in it and spell it *encyclopaedia*. However, *encyclopedia* is the much more common way of spelling it, and it's also easier!

FICTION

A story that has been made up by someone and didn't happen in real life, is a work of *fiction*. Fairy tales are good examples of *fictional* stories.

Fiction v non-fiction

Most books can be described as either *fiction* or *non-fiction*. Books that are about real life and things that exist (or have existed at some point) are *non-fiction*. This book that you are reading right now is an example of *non-fiction*.

ANTHOLOGY

A collection of poems, stories or songs is called an *anthology*. They are often written by different people, but collected together into one book.

BIOGRAPHY

A *biography* is a book that tells the story of a person's life. *Biographies* tend to be written about people who are famous for something, such as celebrities, politicians or figures from history. The writer of a *biography* is called a *biographer*.

Where does it come from?

Bio comes from Greek. When you see it at the start of a word, it usually means that the word relates to life. Other examples include biology (the study of living things) and biopic (a film about someone's life). The *graphy* part of *biography* comes from *graphia*, which means 'writing'.

AUTOBIOGRAPHY

An *autobiography* is also about a person's life, but with one big difference: it is written by the person whose life it is about. If you write a diary, then keep it up. Maybe one day you can turn it into an *autobiography!*

Where does it come from?

Auto means 'self' and *graphia* means 'writing'. So *autobiography* literally means 'writing about yourself'.

ATLAS

A book of maps is called an *atlas*. Some *atlases* show where all the countries of the world are, while others are smaller and more detailed. A *road atlas*, for example, shows maps of where all the roads are in an area.

Did you know?

Atlas was the name of an ancient Greek god, who was made to hold the whole sky on his shoulders. His image was used in early map books, and the name stuck.

SPINE

The line of bones that runs down your back is called your *spine,* and so is the backbone of a book! If you look at the books in a bookshop or library, or even on your own shelves at home, you'll notice that the *spine* is often the only part that is on show. That's why it is important for book *spines* to have information such as the title and the author's name written on them. If it wasn't for their *spines,* books would be a lot harder to find.

Other uses

The sharp, pointy needles you find on cactuses, porcupines and hedgehogs are also called *spines*.

INDEX

An alphabetical list of names, words or topics at the back of a book is called an *index*. *Indexes or indices*[8] can come in very handy if you have a huge book with lots of information in it and you're trying to find one tiny little word. To see

---

[8] Either indexes or indices can correctly be used as the plural of index.

an example of an *index*, turn to the back of the book you're holding right now!

Other uses

The finger next to your thumb (the one you're most likely to use for pointing) is called your *index finger*.

PERFECT PREFIXES

Words that begin with common prefixes – and what they mean.

DECLINE

If you *decline* to do something, you turn down the opportunity to do it. For example, *Joey declined the party invitation because she already had plans.*

Other uses

If an object *declines*, it means it is worsening in quality. If a hill *declines*, it slopes down the way. (Of course, all hills slope both upwards and downwards, depending on which direction you're headed in!).

The prefix part

The prefix is the part at the start of the word, so here it's *de*. It usually indicates that things are going down or away, or being broken apart.

DECIPHER

When you *decipher* something you crack a code or message and work out what it means.

Cipher is another word for a secret code, so if you *decipher* something you reverse the code and get down to what it really means.

Other examples

Some other common *de* words include decompose, degrade and decrease.

BIANNUAL

Something happening twice a year is *biannual*. Alternatively, if something happens just once a year, it is said to be *annual*.

Not to be confused with...

Biennial (something that happens once every two years).

The prefix part

The *bi* prefix means 'two' or 'twice'.

BIPLANE

A *biplane* is an aeroplane with two long wings – one stacked above the other. Biplanes are a bit old-fashioned now, but they still look very cool.

Other examples

Other common *bi* words include bicycle, bifocal and binocular.

> ### Did you know?
> Way back in 1903, brothers Wilbur and Orville Wright flew the first successful aeroplane – which was a *biplane* made of wood.

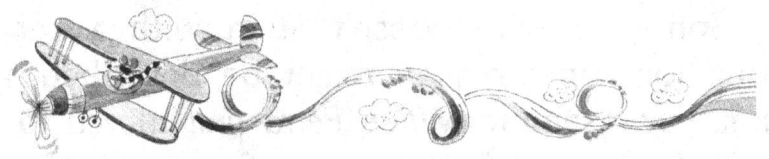

MISSHAPEN

When something is *misshapen*, it doesn't have its normal *shape*. It may have been damaged or poorly made. If you see a funny-looking carrot, you might describe it as *misshapen*.

The prefix part

The *mis* prefix means that something has gone wrong – in this case, the *shape*.

Spellcheck

Most words with the *mis* prefix have a single s, but because shape also starts with an s, there's a double s here. *Misshapen* is pronounced 'miss-shay-pen'.

Not to be confused with...

Mishap (an accident – pronounced 'miss-hap').

MISFIT

Someone who doesn't *fit* in with a certain group for some reason might be described as a *misfit*. For example, *When Petra first moved to her new school she felt like a bit of a misfit, but she soon made lots of friends.*

Other examples

Other *mis* words include misprint, mistrial and mistake.

ANTICLIMAX

Have you ever felt that something was a lot less exciting than you expected it to be? Maybe you've been looking forward to a big sports event, for example, but it turns out to be really boring? That's called an *anticlimax*.

The prefix part

Anti at the start of a word means 'against' or 'opposite'. So an *anticlimax* is the opposite of a *climax*, which is an exciting ending.

ANTIHERO

When the main character in a story doesn't behave like a hero, they could be described as an *antihero*. *Antiheroes* aren't the same as villains, because they aren't evil like villains. However, the *anti* part shows that they go against what you might expect from a traditional *hero*.

Other examples

Some other *anti* words you probably know are antifreeze, antisocial and antidote.

DISSIMILAR

Two things that are different from each other are *dissimilar*. *Dissimilar* is the opposite of similar. For example, *My neighbour and his brother look very dissimilar; one is bald, and the other is very hairy.*

The prefix part

When the *dis* prefix appears, you can usually reverse the meaning of the word that follows after it. So, when *dis* is placed at the start of *similar*, it creates a new word that means 'not similar'.

DISSECT

If you *dissect* something, you cut it up and examine it. In some schools, students are asked to *dissect* dead frogs in their biology lessons. However, you can also *dissect* a film or a book by studying it closely.

Other examples

Other *dis* words include disconnect, disgrace and distrust.

SUBMARINE

A *submarine* is a ship that goes underwater, but the word can also be used to describe anything that is below the surface of the sea.

The prefix part

Sub means 'under' or 'nearly'. With *submarine*, it means 'under the sea' because *marine* describes anything relating to the sea.

> ### Did you know?
>
> A *submarine* is also a kind of sandwich! It doesn't go underwater, though. It's called a *submarine* because of its long shape.

SUBURB

An area outside the centre of a town or city is a *suburb*. You might also hear these areas being described as *suburbia* or *suburban*.

Break it down

Urb is short for *urban*, which relates to the city, so *suburb* means 'nearly in the city' or, to put it another way, 'close to the city'.

Other examples

Here are some other *sub* words: subway, submerge and subdue.

COWORKER

People who *work* with or alongside each other are called *coworkers*. *Coworker* has a similar meaning to colleague.

The prefix part

When used as a prefix, *co* means 'together'. So *coworkers* are people who *work* together.

COEXIST

When two things *exist* at the same time or in the same place, they are said to *coexist*. Coexist is often used when talking about things that *exist* peacefully and in harmony with each other. Bees and flowers are a great example of how insects and plants *coexist*. Bees need flowers because they use their pollen to make honey. Flowers need bees to pollinate them so that they can create seeds.

Other examples

The *co* prefix is also used on coauthor, cocreate and cooperate (pronounced 'koe-op-er-ate').

AUTOMOBILE

Automobile, a word most commonly used in the US, is another word for a car.

The prefix part

Auto means 'self'. *Mobile* means 'to move'. So, an *automobile* is something that can move itself. (As long as someone is there to drive it, that is!)

AUTONOMY

If you control something by yourself, without being told what to do or being influenced by anyone else, you have autonomy. When a country governs itself, without being ruled over by somewhere else, it is *autonomous*. Having *autonomy* is similar to having independence.

Where does it come from?

Autonomy comes from the Greek word *autonomos*, meaning 'having its own laws'. *Nomy* on its own is not a word in English, but comes from the Greek *nomos*, which means 'law'.

Other examples

You can also see the auto prefix at the beginning of words like automatic, autopilot and autofocus.

Did you know?

> A car that can drive itself, without the need for a human driver, is called an *autonomous vehicle*. So even automobiles can have *autonomy!*

TRANSMIT

If you *transmit*, you send data or messages from one place to another. TV and radio shows are *transmitted* to your devices, for example. Diseases are also said to be *transmitted* when passed from one person to another.

The prefix part

When you see *trans* at the start of a word, it usually means 'across' or 'change'. Traditionally, when a TV show was *transmitted*, it was being sent 'across' the airwaves to reach people's televisions.

TRANSLATE

If you change words from one language to another, you *translate* them. For example, *When we visited France, my friend translated the menus for us.* A translator is someone whose job is to translate words into different languages. The phrase *lost in translation* means that one person has misunderstood another person's meaning.

This can happen even when both people are using the same language.

Other examples

Other *trans* words include transfer, transit and transact.

PREDICT

If you *predict* something, you are saying it will happen before it happens, sort of like a forecast. For example, *Hannah predicted that her* brother would win the race, as he had trained so hard.

The prefix part

Pre as a prefix means 'before', 'ahead' or 'in advance of'.

Break it down

Dict is an old-fashioned term meaning 'to say'. It's not used much these days, but it still pops up in other words that relate to words and speaking, such as diction, dictate and contradict.

PRECEDE

To *precede* is to come before something. In a storm, lightning *precedes* thunder, because it comes first. If you and a friend go into a room and you walk in first, you are *preceding* your friend.

Where does it come from?

The *cede* part comes from the Latin *cedere*, meaning 'to move'. So, with the *pre* prefix added on to the start, it literally means 'move before'.

Other examples

Pre also appears at the start of prepare, prevent and, of course, prefix.

POSTPONE

If you *postpone* an event, you move it to a later date. For example, *Sharan had to postpone her party because her shower was leaking.*

The prefix part

Post at the start of a word usually means 'after' or 'later'.

Postpone v cancel

A *postponed* event still happens, but at another time. A cancelled event just gets scrapped completely.

POSTERIOR

Your *posterior* literally comes after you — it's your bottom!

Other uses

Technically, *posterior* can mean anything that comes behind or at the back of something. But mainly it's your bottom!

Other examples

Some other words with the *post* prefix include postgraduate, postmortem and postwar.

> ### Did you know?
> The opposite of *posterior* is anterior, which means 'at the front'.

UNICORN

A *unicorn* is a mythical creature that looks like a horse, but has one horn growing from its forehead. You've probably seen loads of *unicorns* in books, movies and TV shows.

The prefix part

Uni at the start of a word means 'one'.

Where does it come from?

The *uni* at the start of *unicorn* refers to its one horn. But why isn't it called a 'unihorn' instead of a *unicorn*? It's because it comes from Latin, where the word for 'horn' is *cornu*.

UNIVERSITY

A *university* is a school where students can go to continue their education and learn more about the subjects they are most interested in. The *uni* part here is because a *university* is 'one' whole group of students and teachers.

Other examples

Other *uni* words include uniform, universe and unicycle.

IN SICKNESS & IN HEALTH

Words about your body, when it's well and when it's not to so well.

PHYSICAL

Anything that relates to the body, rather than the mind, is *physical*. Your skin and bones, for example, are *physical*, but your thoughts and emotions are mental. *Physical exercise*, such as running or taking part in a sport, keeps your body fit and can help you to stay healthy.

Other uses

Anything that can be touched is also *physical*. *Physical* can also be short for *physical examination*, which is where a person's fitness is tested. For example, *Sabir had to pass a physical before being offered the job.*

INJURY

If a person or animal has an *injury*, they have been hurt or harmed in some way. For example, *The squirrel was taken to the animal hospital after suffering an injury.*

BRUISE

A *bruise* is an injury that doesn't break the skin, but leaves a colourful mark afterwards. *Bruises* can be very sore to touch. For example, Cass *was left with a big bruise on her leg after she fell off her bike.*

MUSCLE

Muscles are pieces of tissue that people and animals have lots of inside their bodies. It's because of *muscles* that you are able to move around. When a person does lots of exercise such as weightlifting, their *muscles* can become bigger. If someone is described as having *lots of muscle*, it means they are very strong. However, strong people have the same number of *muscles* as everyone else.

> **Did you know?**
> Your body has over 600 muscles!

Not to be confused with...

Mussel (a shellfish that clings to rocks).

BICEPS

The muscle at the front of your upper arm is called your *biceps*. The word is always *biceps*, whether you are talking about one *biceps* or lots of *biceps*. You might hear people use the word 'bicep', but this is actually incorrect.

STOMACH

When you swallow food, it goes down to an organ inside your body called your *stomach* to be digested. You might know it as your 'belly' or 'tummy', but stomach is the proper word for it. If you eat too much or you feel nervous about something, you might suffer from *stomachache*, which is a pain in your tummy.

Other uses

If you don't like something, you might say you can't *stomach* it or *don't have the stomach for it.* For example, *Gabriel knew he was right, but he had no stomach for an argument.*

> ### Did you know?
> It's often said that cows have four stomachs. In fact, they only have one stomach, but it has four compartments.

NAVEL

Your *navel* is the knobbly little mark you have just below your waist. You probably know your *navel* better as your belly button. Some belly buttons stick out and some go in, but everyone has one.

Not to be confused with...

Naval (something that relates to a navy, such as a *naval officer* or a *naval base*).

SYMPTOM

A *symptom* is a sign that a person is unwell. For example, a runny nose is a *symptom* of a cold. If you visit a doctor because you feel ill, the doctor will ask what your *symptoms* are so that they can figure out what might be wrong with you.

Other uses

Anything that is caused by a bad situation could be described as *a symptom. For example,*

The bad turn out at the concert was a symptom of the terrible weather.

FRACTURE

A *fracture* is another word for a broken bone. For example, *The X-ray showed that Carlos had fractured his arm.* A small crack in a bone is sometimes called a *hairline fracture,* because it is thin like a strand of hair.

Other uses

When a group or organization splits or breaks up, it could be described as *fractured*. For example, if two friends fall out and they stop talking to each other, their friendship is *fractured*.

Not to be confused with...

Fractious (to quickly become upset or angry).

PHOBIA

An extreme fear or hatred of something is called a *phobia*. Often, people have phobias of things that are unlikely to cause them any harm. A very common one is *arachnophobia*, which is the fear of spiders. Spiders are nearly always more scared of people than people are of them, but that doesn't make them any less scary to an *arachnophobe!*

Where does it come from?

Phobia comes from *phobos*, which is Greek for 'fear'. *Phobias* usually have a longer name that describes the specific thing that the person is afraid of.

Ten phobias you might not have heard of
- *Pogonophobia* – the fear of beards
- *Anthophobia* – the fear of flowers
- *Genuphobia* – the fear of knees
- *Nephophobia* – the fear of clouds
- *Papyrophobia* – the fear of paper
- *Octophobia* – the fear of the number eight
- *Chorophobia* – the fear of dancing
- *Alektorophobia* – the fear of chickens
- *Anthropophobia* – the fear of people
- *Phobophobia* – the fear of phobias!

DEHYDRATION

Dehydration is when most or all of the water is removed from something. If you don't drink enough water, you'll become *dehydrated*. *Dehydration* can make you feel dizzy, sick and, of course, very thirsty.

Break it down

If you *hydrate* something, you add water or moisture to it. The de prefix turns this around, and means you take water away. The *hydra* part comes from *hydro*, which always relates to water. Hydroelectricity, for example, is electricity generated by running water.

Did you know?

Humans can survive for more than three weeks with no food, but only around one week with no water. So drinking water is very important! It's suggested that people should drink six to eight glasses of water every day to avoid becoming *dehydrated*.

DIARRHOEA

When you have to rush to the toilet because your poo is very runny, you have *diarrhoea* (pronounced 'dy-ah-ree-ah'). *Diarrhoea* is usually a symptom of another illness, and can cause dehydration.

Spellcheck

Diarrhoea isn't just difficult to deal with ... it's also hard to spell. It might help to remember the first letters of each word in this fitting phrase: **d**ash in **a r**eal rush, **h**urry **o**r **e**lse **a**ccident.

ALLERGY

If you have an *allergy* to something, your body reacts to it and becomes uncomfortable when you touch it, eat it, smell it or even just go near it. You might get a rash, a runny nose or itchy eyes. In really bad cases, an *allergic reaction* can cause the sufferer to become unconscious or even die. People can be *allergic* to all sorts of things, but common *allergens* (things that cause *allergies*) include pollen, nuts and seafood.

Other uses

People sometimes use *allergy* as another word for a strong dislike. For example, *Mum said Freddie didn't clean his room because he was allergic to hard work.*

ANTIBIOTIC

An *antibiotic* is a kind of medicine. It works by killing bacteria in your body that could be making you ill.

Break it down

Anti means 'against' and biotic refers to living things (in this case, the bacteria). You may also have heard of probiotics. Probiotics do the opposite: they help your body to grow the good kind of bacteria that helps you to stay healthy.

MONEY, MONEY, MONEY

Words about saving, spending and shopping.

MINT

The factory where coins are made is called a *mint*. Because of this, *mint* has also become a slang term for a lot of money. That's why you might sometimes hear people using phrases like *I've made a mint* or *I'm minted*, if they've come into a large amount of money. If something is brand new and unused, it might be described as being in *mint condition* – just like the shiny new coins that leave the mint.

Other uses

Mint is also a green herb that is used to make things such as peppermints and toothpaste.

DEPOSIT

When you pay a small amount of money to buy something, with the intention of paying the rest of the price at a later date, that first payment is called a *deposit*.

Other uses

Deposit can also mean to put something in a place. When you put money into your bank account, for example, you are making a *deposit*. You could also *deposit* your valuables in a safe. A *deposit* might also be something left behind by a process, such as the soil or rock *deposits* left by rivers.

BANKRUPT

If a person (or business) has gone *bankrupt*, it means that they have no money left to pay the money they owe.

Where does it come from?

The *bank* part is obvious, but what about the rest of it? *Rupt* is short for *ruptus*, which is a Latin word meaning 'to break'. So *bankrupt* literally means that your bank is broken.

LOAN

If you borrow something from someone, they are giving you a loan or 'lending' it to you. It's not yours, though, so you have to give it back. The same thing applies to money. When money is received as a *loan*, it has to be paid back.

Not to be confused with...

Lone (someone or something on their own). For example, *A lone tree stood on a hill*. The 'one' at the end should help you to remember this. If there's only **one** of something, it's **lone.**

SALARY

The money that a person is regularly paid for doing their job is called a *salary*. Normally, a person who has a *salary* will receive the same amount of money with each payment, which could be given to them either every week or every month.

Salary v wage

These two words are very similar in meaning, as both refer to a payment for doing a job. The main difference is that *salary* payments are usually the same fixed amount each time. A wage, on the other hand, might go up or down depending on how many hours a person has worked.

Where does it come from?

The word salary comes from the Latin *salarium*, which means 'money for salt'. It's thought that this is because Roman soldiers were partly paid in salt instead of money – but a lot of historians disagree with this!

TAX

Money that people pay to the government, so that it can pay for services such as hospitals, schools and roads, is called *tax*. There are lots of different types of *tax*. Some *tax* is added on to the value of goods in shops. Other *tax* is taken directly out of the money that people are paid for doing their jobs.

Not to be confused with...

Tacks (short nails with flat tops, used to hold things in place).

CURRENCY

You might have noticed that different countries of the world have different names for their money. That isn't just because they sometimes speak different languages. Each country's money is called its *currency*. For example, in the UK pounds (written with a '£' symbol) are used, while in the US dollars (written as '$') are used. Sometimes, countries share the same *currency*. Lots of countries in Europe, for example, use a *currency* called the euro (written as '€').

Other uses

If lots of people agree that something has value, it is said to *have currency*. For example, *The plan to create a new park in the middle of town had currency with the locals.*

EXCHANGE

When you swap one item for another, you *exchange* it. When talking about money, it means to swap one currency for another. So, if you live in the UK and you're going on a trip to the US, you would need to exchange some of your pounds for some dollars.

How does it work?

The *exchange rate* is a system that measures one currency against another, so that you know how much you will get back in your *exchange*. For example, £1 might be worth $1.30, so for every £1 you *exchange* you will get $1.30 back. Then you can go and spend all your new dollars on your trip!

CHEAP

If something is *cheap*, then it's low in price, which can be a very good thing for your pocket (*ka-ching!*). But before you rush out to bag that bargain, buyer beware! Sometimes, *cheap* can also be used to describe things that haven't been made very well and are of bad quality.

Is it good or bad?

Is your bargain buy *cheap and cheerful* or *cheap and nasty*? Both are inexpensive, but one does its job well while the other one is very probably a mess.

Not to be confused with...

Cheep (the high, squeaky noise baby birds make).

BARGAIN

When something costs a lot less than you'd expect it to, it's called a *bargain*. For example, *Lauren waited until the sales were on and grabbed herself a great bargain.*

Other uses

Bargains don't necessarily involve money. When two people make an agreement that involves each of them doing something for the other, that could also be called a *bargain*. Making this kind of agreement is often called *striking a bargain*. Someone who asks a lot from this kind of arrangement could be said to be *driving a hard bargain.*

DISCOUNT

When the price of something is reduced, the amount it is reduced by is called a *discount.* For example, if a person works in a shop, they might be allowed to buy things from the shop at a lower price. That is called a *staff discount.*

Other uses

Discount can also mean to disregard something. For example, *When Jack was told that aliens had landed in his town, he decided to discount it as untrue.*

REFUND

If you are unhappy with something you buy and you return it to get your money back, the returned money is called a *refund.*

Where does it come from?

Refund comes from the Latin *refundere,* where *re* means 'back' and *fundere* means 'to pour'. Think about how, in English, *fund* means to provide money for something. Well, *refund* means that the money has been provided, but then it has been given back.

GUARANTEE

A *guarantee* is a kind of promise. If someone says they *guarantee* something, they are saying that it will definitely happen. So, if you buy a new TV that comes with a ten-year *guarantee*, the *guarantee* is a promise that the TV will last for at least ten years. If the TV stops working before the ten years are up, you can get a free replacement or your money back.

Guarantee v warranty

These two words sound similar, and are often confused. A warranty is the written agreement that confirms a *guarantee*.

CONVENIENCE

A *convenience* is something that makes life easier or more comfortable. *Convenience shops* or *stores* do this, because they sell bits and pieces that you might need at short notice (such as milk or bread), and they're often open late.

Other uses

Modern *conveniences* are things like dishwashers and washing machines. They make life easier by performing jobs that people used to have to do by hand.

Did you know?

Public convenience is a fancy name for a public toilet. It makes sense, when you think about it. If you're out somewhere and you need to pee, then a public toilet is very *convenient!*

WEATHER WORDS

Words you can use, rain or shine.

CLIMATE

The usual weather conditions of a place are known as its *climate*. For example, the Sahara has a hot *desert climate* and the UK has a *temperate climate*. 'Temperate' means it gets neither really hot nor really cold.

Changing times

The change in the Earth's *climate*, particularly its rising temperature due to higher levels of gases such as carbon dioxide, is called *climate change*. The term is mainly used when talking about the ways in which humans have contributed to global warming.

Other uses

The general mood somewhere can also be described as its *climate*. For example, *political climate* refers to the way people in an area feel about politics.

Climatic v climactic

Be careful with that extra *c*. *Climatic* refers to the *climate*. 'Climactic' refers to the final exciting moment in a story or event, otherwise known as the 'climax'.

PRECIPITATION

In weather terms, *precipitation* is the scientific word for rain, snow, sleet or hail. You probably wouldn't look out the window, see that it's raining and say, *Look at all the precipitation!* But technically you would be correct if you did.

DRIZZLE

Drizzle is the very lightest of rains. Rain isn't the only thing that *drizzles*, though. You can *drizzle* a dressing over salad, or syrup over pancakes. To *drizzle* means to drip or dribble just a small amount over something. So, if you like a lot of syrup on your pancakes, you'll probably want to use a different word.

> **Did you know?**
>
> A *drizzle cake* is a sponge cake with a syrup poured over the top of it to make a light glaze. *Lemon drizzle* cake is a particularly tasty one!

MONSOON

Monsoon is often used to describe any heavy rainfall, but technically it refers to the seasons that bring lots of rain to parts of Southern Asia, Africa, Australia and Central America. When the wind changes direction in the winter, it brings dry weather, and becomes a *dry monsoon*.

DROUGHT

When a place has no rainfall for a long time, it is said to be having a *drought*. In extreme cases, *droughts* can be very dangerous. When there is no rain, places can run out of water, meaning plants can't grow and people and animals can't get food. A long period with no available food is called a famine.

> **Did you know?**
>
> The word *drought* used to be used to describe thirst.

MIST

When lots of tiny droplets of water in the air make it hard to see, the visible clouds formed are called *mist*. So, what's the difference between mist and fog? Well, fog is much denser than *mist*. Technically, if you can see less than 1,000 metres ahead of you, it is fog rather than mist. There is also haze, which is similarly hard to see through, but usually forms in hot, dry air.

Not to be confused with...

Missed (failing to hit, as in, *Rachel missed the target*; or noticing the absence of something, as in, *After Jin left school, everyone said he would be missed*).

HURRICANE

A *hurricane* is an especially powerful storm. The speed of winds in a *hurricane* is faster than most cars will ever drive, which means they are very violent and destructive.

Spellcheck

To remember the two *r*'s in **hurr**i**c**ane, think of being in a 'hur**r** **hurry**' to get out of the way.

TORNADO

A *tornado* is a fast-moving column of air that spins round and round, causing a lot of damage. *Tornadoes* can uproot trees, destroy buildings and even pick up cars!

Did you know?

Tornadoes are very difficult to study, as they can often demolish any measuring equipment that gets in their way. Because of this, scientists aren't completely sure how they are formed. 'Storm chasers' are people who literally chase after *tornadoes* and other dangerous storms, often to try to learn more about them. How about that for an exciting (and dangerous) job?

TYPHOON

A *typhoon* is a violent tropical storm that typically happens in the western Pacific or Indian oceans.

Where does it come from?

Typhoon comes from the Chinese *tai fung*, meaning *great wind*.

TSUNAMI

A *tsunami* is an enormous and very powerful wave, often caused by an earthquake or a volcanic eruption. One of the most recent destructive *tsunamis* occurred in the Indian Ocean in 2004. Some waves were up to 30 metres high and caused a huge amount of damage in many surrounding countries.

Where does it come from?

Tsunami is a Japanese word, pronounced with a silent *t* as 'soo-nah-mee'. *Tsu* means 'harbour' and *nami* means 'wave'.

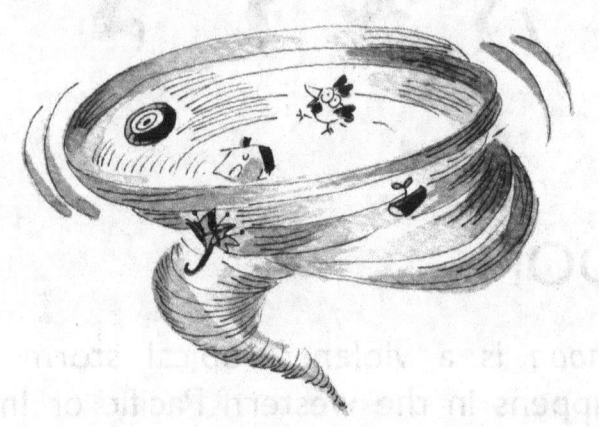

LIGHTNING

If you've ever experienced a thunderstorm, then you've probably seen these bright flashes of light in the sky. *Lightning* is a burst of electricity – exactly the same as the electricity you use to charge your devices at home. The shorter the gap between the sound of thunder and a bolt of *lightning,* the closer you are to the storm. If they happen at the same time, take cover!

Other uses

Lightning can mean 'very fast'. People sometimes describe sports stars as being *lightning quick* or having *lightning reflexes*.

Not to be confused with...

Lightening (making something lighter).

HUMID

If somewhere is *humid*, it means there is a lot of moisture or dampness in the air, usually combined with a hot temperature. If you've ever visited Southeast Asia or been inside a greenhouse, you may have heard people complaining about it being muggy or *humid*.

Just the opposite

The opposite of *humid* is 'dry' or 'arid'. You might have a *dehumidifier* at home. This is a machine that removes moisture from the air in a room. *Humidity* indoors is bad news, as it can cause mould, which can be an expensive problem to fix.

AVALANCHE

Look out! *Avalanche!* When a large amount of snow, ice and rocks dislodges and slides quickly down a mountainside, it's called an *avalanche*.

Other uses

Avalanche can also be used to describe anything that happens without much warning and has a massive impact. For example, We've *had an avalanche of competition entries* or *The soccer game had an avalanche of goals.*

Where does it come from?

Avalanche has an odd spelling because it comes from French. It's pronounced 'ahv-ah-lanch'.

ISOBAR

Ever seen the weather forecast on TV and wondered what all those wiggly lines on the map are? They are called *isobars*. They show and connect the places that have the same atmospheric pressure at a certain time. Areas connected by an *isobar* will probably experience similar weather conditions. As the weather changes, the positions of the *isobars* may move and change too.

Did you know?

There are also lines called isotherms, which are similar to *isobars* but link places where the temperature is the same. There are isohyets, too. These connect places that have the same amount of rainfall.

BY THE NUMBERS

Words about numbers, shapes and mathematics.

ARITHMETIC

If you add, subtract, multiply or divide numbers, you are doing *arithmetic*. It's what you use when you're doing any sums. For example, *Padma was very good with numbers and arithmetic.*

Spellcheck

You pronounce *arithmetic* the same way that you spell it ('ah-rith-meh-tick'). The only trouble is, it's difficult to spell. Remembering the first letters of this phrase might help you: **a** **r**at **i**n **t**he **h**ouse **m**ay **e**at **t**he **i**ce **c**ream.

ALGEBRA

Algebra is where letters or other symbols are used in place of numbers. When you see a sum that has a letter in it instead of a number, the aim is to work out what number needs to be swapped in for the letter. Here's a very simple example of *algebra*. Can you work out what number the letter y represents? The answer is at the bottom of the page opposite.

4 + 3 + y = 12
y = 5 (of course!)

Where does it come from?

The word *algebra* comes from the Arabic word *al-jabr*, which loosely translates as 'put broken parts back together'. When you think about it, that's sort of what *algebra* does. By working out the value of the letters you're fixing the broken parts of the sum.

PERCENT

One *percent* (often written with a % symbol) is one part of a hundred parts. The total amount of something is always 100 percent, and from that you can work out the *percentage* value of smaller amounts. For example, if a whole pie is 100 *percent*, then half of that pie is 50 *percent* and a quarter is 25 *percent*.

Break it down

The word *per* is used to show a ratio. For example, *Sally was paid her money per hour instead of per week.* Where you see *cent*, it's usually connected to the number 100. For example, there are 100 *cents* in a dollar and 100 years in a *century*. Smash the meanings of *per* and *cent* together and you get *percent*: the amount of something *per* 100.

Where does it come from?

Both *per* and *cent* come from Latin. *Per* means 'by' or 'through' and *centum* means 'hundred'.

AVERAGE

In mathematics, you work out the *average* of a group of numbers by adding those numbers together and dividing the result by the number of numbers in the group. Make sense? An example will probably help! If you have the numbers 1, 2, 3, 4 and 5, you add them together and get 15. Then you divide 15 by 5 (because you added a group of five numbers together), and you get 3. So 3 is the *average*.

Other uses

Because the *average* number tends to be somewhere in the middle, people also use the word *average* to describe things that are neither good nor bad, but somewhere in between. For example, *Erhun said the food in the restaurant was average.*

SYMMETRY

When two halves of something are the same on both sides, they have *symmetry*. Lots of shapes are *symmetrical*, such as squares and circles, because if you fold them down the middle they meet perfectly on both sides. *Symmetry* exists in nature, too. Many butterflies, for example, have *symmetrical* wing patterns.

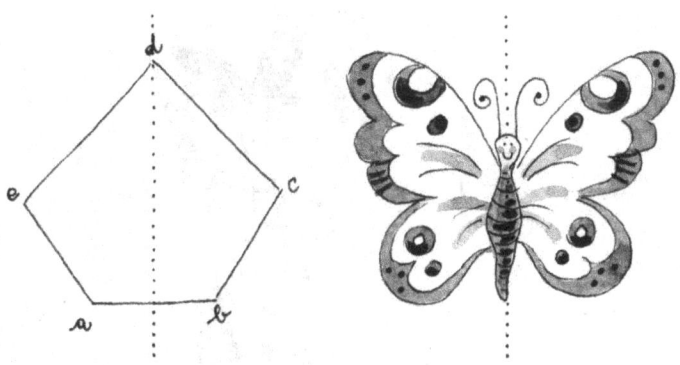

ACUTE

An *acute* angle is an angle of less than 90 degrees (so it is pointy and sharp).

Other uses

In medicine, an *acute illness* is one that is severe, but doesn't last long. If someone describes their pain as *acute*, it means the pain is sharp or intense. *Acute* can also mean 'shrewd'. If you have an acute *awareness* of something, you understand it very well indeed. In the same way, if you have an *acute sense of smell*, it means that your sense of smell is excellent.

Not to be confused with...

A cute (as in, what a cute puppy!).

OBTUSE

An angle that is between 90 and 180 degrees is described as *obtuse*. If an angle is exactly 90 degrees, it is called a right angle (so is neither *obtuse* nor acute).

Other uses

A person who is slow to understand things could be described as *obtuse*.

ARC

An *arc* is a curved line. If an *arc* is so long that its two ends join up together, it stops being an *arc* and becomes a circle.

Not to be confused with...

Ark (the boat used by Noah to escape the Flood in the Bible).

CIRCUMFERENCE

The distance measured around the edge of a circle is called its *circumference*.

Where does it come from?

Circumference originally comes from the Latin word *circumferre*, where *circum* means 'around' and *ferre* means 'to carry or bear'.

Did you know?

The *circumference* of the Earth at its equator is around 40,075 kilometres. However, the *circumference* going through its poles is slightly shorter, at 40,008 kilometres. That's because the Earth is not a perfect sphere.

RADIUS

If you draw a straight line from the edge of a circle to its centre, and then measure that line, the measurement is the circle's *radius*.

Other uses

You also have a bone in your arm called the *radius bone*. It's the shorter of the two bones that go from your elbow to your wrist.

Where does it come from?

Radius is the Latin word for a 'rod, spoke or ray'. The spoke of a bicycle wheel gives a great demonstration of a *radius*, as it starts in the middle of a circle and goes out to the edge.

DIAMETER

The distance right across a circle, through the middle and from one edge to the other, is its *diameter*. With a perfect circle, the *diameter* is always double the length of the radius.

Break it down

To find the *diameter*, you 'measure through' the centre of the circle. *Dia* means 'through' and *meter* means 'measure'. That's why *meter* is often found in the names of measuring devices, such as thermometers (for measuring temperature) and barometers (for measuring air pressure).

OPERATION

An *operation* is an activity or process. In mathematics, an *operation* is the action of doing something to a number, such as adding, subtracting, multiplying or dividing it.

Other uses

Surgeons in hospitals perform operations on their patients. An *operation* can also be another word for a business. If a machine is in *operation*, it means that it is in use.

PRIME

A *prime number* is a whole number that can only be perfectly divided by itself and the number

1. Examples of *prime numbers* are 2, 3, 5, 7, 11, 13 and 17.

Other uses

Prime can also mean the best or most important. A shop might be in *a prime location*, a healthy person might be considered to be in the *prime of their life*, and a country might be led by a *prime minister*. A *prime example* is something that is an excellent example. *The number two is a prime example of a prime number!*

Pi

If you divide any circle's circumference by its diameter, you'll get the number 3.142, which is known as pi. Pi is sometimes written as the symbol π, which originally comes from the Greek alphabet.

Not to be confused with...

Pie (a pastry-based food, which is pronounced in the same way as *pi* but is a lot tastier).

You'll usually see *pi* rounded to a few decimal places (for example, when written as 3.142, it has been rounded to three places after the decimal point). However, the true number of decimal places goes on forever! Scientists have worked out over 30 trillion decimal places for *pi* so far, but it keeps going way beyond that.

INFINITE

Something that is *infinite* goes on forever. The number of decimal places in pi are *infinite*, because they never come to an end. The surface of a globe could be thought of as *infinite*, because you can go round and round it forever and never reach an edge. Time is also *infinite*, because time will never end!

Just the opposite

Infinite is the opposite of *finite*. If something is *finite*, it has an edge or boundary. *Finite* comes from the Latin *finitus*, which means 'finish'.

ARE THEY EVEN REAL WORDS?

Words to make you laugh.

DISCOMBOBULATE

This is a really complicated way of saying 'confuse'. If you're struggling to complete a particularly difficult puzzle, you might describe yourself as *discombobulated*. You might also say it if you get lost on your way somewhere. For example, *Samia gave me directions to her house, but I got all turned round and discombobulated.*

Puzzling prefix

You can be *discombobulated*, but it's not possible to just be 'combobulated' – because that's not a real word.

GOBBLEDEGOOK

When someone uses language that is so complicated that it becomes impossible to understand, you could call it *gobbledegook*. Another word for *gobbledegook* is 'jargon'. For example, *The computer expert used so much technical gobbledegook that I completely switched off.*

Where does it come from?

Gobbledegook is a relatively new word that was first used in the 1940s. It's thought that the word was probably intended to compare confusing language to a turkey's 'gobble' sound, as both are impossible to understand.

EGGHEAD

An *egghead* is someone who is a highly educated expert, and possibly even a genius. The word is commonly thought to come from the idea that a very clever person must have a very big brain (so also a big head). In reality, of course, cleverness has no connection to head size.

Other uses

An *egghead* can also be someone who doesn't use a picture of their own on certain social media sites. Instead, they use the original egg-like picture that was supplied when they signed up.

COLLYWOBBLES

If you're experiencing *collywobbles*, it means you have a stomachache or a feeling of nervousness in your tummy.

Where does it come from?

The *colly* part is thought to probably be short for either colic or cholera. Both are nasty illnesses that can affect you in the tummy department.

DOPPELGÄNGER

A *doppelgänger* is a person who looks eerily like someone else. Ever met another person who looked exactly like you? Did it totally freak you out? *Doppelgängers* have a habit of doing that. Seeing one can be a confusing experience — especially when it's your own *doppelgänger*.

Where does it come from?

While it's now used in English, the word is actually German and literally means 'double-goer'.

What's that funny symbol?

The two dots on top of the *ä* form a symbol called an 'umlaut'. In German, umlauts are sometimes used over vowels to change the way they sound.

VAMOOSE

Vamoose means to leave somewhere quickly. For example, *Come on, everyone, we're running late – vamoose!*

Where does it come from?

Sadly, *vamoose* has nothing to do with the animal 'moose' or with the dessert 'mousse'! *Vamoose* comes from the Spanish word *vamos*, meaning 'let's go'.

WIDDERSHINS

Widdershins is an old-fashioned way of saying 'counter-clockwise' or 'in the opposite direction'.

Where does it come from?

Widdershins comes originally from Scotland, with *widder* meaning 'against', and *shins* meaning 'direction'. It has nothing to do with the shins on your legs.

DIDDLY-SQUAT

If a person says they know *diddly-squat* about something, it means they know nothing about it. And if they're doing *diddly-squat*, then it means they're not doing very much at all. For example,

When Kim was tidying up, her brother did diddly-squat to help.

Where does it come from?

Diddly-squat is originally a US term, dating back to the 1960s. You might sometimes see it written as *doodly-squat* or even just *diddly*.

RAGAMUFFIN

There's no muffin connection with this one, so try not to lick your lips. Originally, *ragamuffin* was a word for a child with dirty or ragged clothes. Nowadays, it's used for anyone who looks dishevelled or scruffy. For example, *Dad said that when he picked me up from school I looked like a ragamuffin!*

Similar meaning, different word

Another funny old-fashioned word for a scruffy child is a 'guttersnipe'. Guttersnipes also tend to be badly behaved and spend most of their time out on the street.

Other uses

Ragamuffin is also often associated with ragga music, but notice that there are two g's in ragga. Ragga is a music style that comes from the Caribbean. It is similar to rap and derived from reggae.

CODSWALLOP

Ever heard the phrase *What a load of old codswallop?* It's a slang way of saying that something is nonsense. For example, *Mia said the dog ate her homework, but the teacher knew she was talking codswallop!*

Where does it come from?

There's a popular story that *codswallop* was a soft drink created in the 19th century by a drinks maker called Hiram Codd. At the time, wallop was a slang term used for beer, so Codd's alternative drink became known as *codswallop*. However, many believe this story is, in itself, complete *codswallop!*

GARGOYLE

A *gargoyle* is a strange, ugly stone carving of a creature. You'll often see *gargoyles* if you look up towards the roofs of really old buildings.

Where does it come from?

The word *gargoyle* comes from the French word *gargouille*, meaning 'throat'. That's because water often drains through the throat of a *gargoyle*. The word 'gargle' – meaning to rinse out your mouth and throat – comes from the same place.

BALDERDASH

If you think that something is ridiculous and untrue, you could call it *balderdash*. For example, *Jamie made up a mean story about Greta, but everyone knew that it was balderdash.*

Where does it come from?

No one is entirely sure of *balderdash's* origins, but it could come from the Welsh word *baldorddus*, which means 'chatter or noisy talk'.

BAFFLEGAB

Bafflegab has a similar meaning to gobbledegook and jargon. It refers to language that is confusing, even when it doesn't need to be. For example, *The instructions for our new laptop were a load of bafflegab.*

WINKLE-PICKER

A *winkle-picker* is a shoe with a sharp, pointy toe. It might seem odd now, but back in the 1950s *winkle-pickers* were a big fashion craze.

Where does it come from?

Winkle is short for *periwinkle*, which is the name of a small sea snail. Traditionally, *winkles* were eaten by using a narrow pin to 'pick' the snail out of its shell. *Winkle-picker* shoes are so pointy at the front that they were named after those winkle-picking pins!

BAMBOOZLE

To *bamboozle* someone is to confuse them, or even cheat or trick them. For example, *The burglar hoped to bamboozle the police by wearing a disguise.*

Where does it come from?

No one is entirely sure of *bamboozle's* origins, but it's known to date back several hundred years at least. It may come from the Scottish word *bumbaze,* which also means 'to confuse', and could easily have made it into this chapter too!

FIDDLESTICKS

Fiddlesticks is something you might say when you're annoyed. It's best written with an exclamation mark at the end, to really emphasize just how annoyed you are. For example, *I left my packed lunch at home again. Fiddlesticks!*

Did you know?

A *fiddlestick* is a very old-fashioned term for the bow that is used to play a violin (which is also known as a *fiddle*).

GAZUMP

If you buy something that has already been promised to someone else, then you *gazump* them. This word is used a lot when people are buying houses. If someone has agreed to buy a house but someone else comes along and offers more money for it, then the first person is in danger of being *gazumped*. It might be a funny word, but it's not a very nice thing to do to someone!

Where does it come from?

Gazump is thought to have come from the Yiddish word *gezumph*, which means 'to overcharge or cheat someone'.

SKULDUGGERY

Dishonest or underhand behaviour is sometimes called *skulduggery*. Note that it has nothing to do with skulls.

POLLIWOG

You probably already know that a tadpole is a tiny creature that turns into a frog. Well, *polliwog* is another name for a tadpole. You might also see it written as *pollywog*. In this case, either spelling is OK to use.

Break it down

Think about other words you know that have *poll* in them. They usually have something to do with voting, as in 'counting heads'. A tax on every person is sometimes called a *poll* tax because it's a tax on every head. With *polliwog*, the *poll* part refers to 'head' too, and the *wog* part is likely to come from 'wiggle'. So, if you think about it, a *polliwog* is a 'head wiggle' – which is actually a pretty accurate description of a tadpole!

Did you know?

Polliwog is also a slang word for a sailor who has never sailed across the equator.

TOUGH TO SPELL

Words that might try to trip you up!

MINUSCULE

Minuscule is a great word for describing things that are very, very teeny-tiny. Unfortunately, it can also be a confusing word, because you'd expect it to have two i's in it, like 'mini'. *Minuscule* is pronounced 'mih-nuh-skyool'.

Spellcheck

Try remembering it this way: *minuscule* things are so small that it's almost as if they are 'minus' something – as in **minus**cule.

SCHEDULE

If you have a busy day ahead, you might come up with a *schedule*. It's a plan for what happens when, usually written as a list.

'Shedule' or 'skedule'?

Actually, both pronunciations are correct. How you say it normally depends on where you were brought up. In the UK, people tend to say 'shedule', while in North America it's usually 'skedule'. However, it's always spelled *schedule*.

EMBARRASS

Everyone has been *embarrassed* at one point or another. It's when something causes you to feel shy or awkward around other people. If you've ever had any *embarrassing* moments, it's best not to think about them!

Spellcheck

Here's an easy way to remember the spelling of this one: *embar***rass** ends with an **ass!**

CONSENSUS

If a group of people come to an agreement on something, it's called a consensus. For example, you might say, *We reached a consensus to watch a comedy movie instead of a thriller.*

Spellcheck

Consensus has one c and three s's. Remember, finding a con**sens**us makes good **sen**se!

PASTIME

What do you like to do to pass the time when you're not at school? Well, that's a *pastime*. A *pastime* could be a hobby, playing a sport or reading. It could be pretty much anything!

Spellcheck

People often think *pastime* is two separate words. After all, when you say it, it sounds like it could be 'pass time' or even 'past time'. But it's just one word: *pastime*.

OCCURRENCE

When something happens, it is called an *occurrence*. For example, *The Sun rising is a daily occurrence.*

Spellcheck

There are a lot of potential pitfalls with the spelling of this word. Remember, there's a double c and a double *r*, and it ends in 'ence', not 'ance'.

COULD

Could is the past tense of 'can' – it's unlikely you've gotten this far without knowing that. But *could*'s tricky spelling and silent *l* sometimes trip people up.

Spellcheck

Remembering this line might help you with the spelling of this one (and 'would' and 'should' too): **oh u lucky duck!**

SEPARATE

When something isn't joined to anything else, we say that it is *separate*. If you do something *separately* to other people, it means you're doing it on your own. For example, you might go to a theme park with friends, but leave *separately* at different times.

Spellcheck

Separate is often mistakenly spelled with an e in the middle where the *a* should be. Try remembering it this way: there is **a rat** in se**parat**e.

DIFFICULTY

A *difficulty* is something that is causing a problem. It could also be a disagreement between two people. For example, *Tanya and her friend were having difficulties.*

Spellcheck

Having *difficulty* remembering how to spell *difficulty*? Try remembering this rhyme:
Mrs **D**, Mrs **I**, Mrs **F F I**,
Mrs **C**, Mrs **U**, Mrs **L T Y!**

BURGLARY

A *burglary* is when someone (a *burglar*) breaks into a place and steals from it.

Spellcheck

Remember: it's just *burglar* with a y on the end. Resist the temptation to go with 'burglery' or 'burgalry'.

INDICT

If someone is charged with a crime (which means the police have officially accused them of doing it), you might say they have been *indicted*. This word is most commonly used in North America.

Silence please

The *c* is completely silent. It's pronounced 'in-dite'.

Not to be confused with...

Indite (a very old and rarely used word that means 'to write').

ASTHMA

Asthma is a health condition that affects people's lungs and can make it hard for them to breathe properly.

Spellcheck

Despite the spelling, it's pronounced 'ass-mah'. Try this trick for remembering the *th* in the middle: someone with *as**th**ma* may have difficulty brea***th***ing.

LIAISON

A *liaison* is a cooperation between people or groups. A *liaison* can also be the person who goes between the two groups to help things along. So, you could say, *When Hugo's two friends fell out, he acted as a liaison to help them sort out their differences.* Good old Hugo!

Spellcheck

The two *i*'s in *liaison* can be tricky to remember. Try thinking about it like this: in l*i**a**i*son, the **a** is liaising between two **i**'s.

MILLIONAIRE

If you're a *millionaire*, you have a lot of money. Over a million pounds (or dollars), in fact.

Spellcheck

Remember: a *millionaire* has lots of loot, but only one **n**.

Just to confuse things...

The word 'questionnaire' might sound very similar, but it has two *n*'s in the middle instead of one. A questionnaire is a list of questions (not a person who has a lot of questions!).

> ### Did you know?
>
> One million is written with six zeros, like this: 1,000,000. A person who has over a billion pounds (or dollars) is a billionaire. One billion is the same as 1,000 million! One billion has nine zeros and is written as 1,000,000,000.

PTERODACTYL

The *pterodactyl* was a huge flying reptile that lived among the dinosaurs, from the late Jurassic period through to the late Cretaceous period (145 million to 65 million years ago). It had a long, narrow beak that it could use to scoop up fish and other prey.

Silence please

The *p* at the beginning is silent, which makes it a particularly 'ptricky' word. *Pterodactyl* is pronounced 'ter-oh-dack-till'. Try remembering that the **pt** at the start could stand for **p**retty **t**errifying.

Ridiculously complicated prehistoric names

What is it with extinct reptiles and dinosaurs and their hard-to-spell names? Here are some others that are tough to spell and even tougher to say!
• Huehuecanauhtlus ('way-way-can-ah oot-luss')
• Epidexipteryx ('ep-ih-dex-ip-teh-ricks')

- Xiongguanlong ('zhong-gwan-long')
- Phlegethontia ('fleg-eh-thon-tee-ah')

BEAUTIFUL

If something is *beautiful,* it means you find it attractive or very pleasant. Pretty much anything can be *beautiful* – a sunrise, a place, a person, a pet or even something that you can't see, such as a piece of music.

Spellcheck

Big elephants aren't ugly! Take the first letter from each of these words to remember the tricky start to the word beau **beau***tiful.*

Did you know?

> You might have heard people use the phrase *beauty is in the eye of the beholder*. This basically means that everyone has their own opinion on what they consider to be *beautiful*.

CALENDAR

A chart showing the days, weeks and months of the year is called a *calendar*. You may have a *calendar* on your wall, on a computer, in a diary or even at special times of the year when you are looking forward to something – such as an *advent calendar* at Christmas, for example.

Spellcheck

People often slip up on the *a* at the end, and mistakenly use an e instead. Try remembering it this way: a c**a**lend**a**r has two *a*'s and two months that start with **A** (**A**pril and **A**ugust).

FRIEND

Someone who you like and know well, but is not part of your family, is called your *friend*. If someone is *friendly* towards you it means they are kind and nice to you.

Spellcheck

Unlike some of the other words in this book, *friend* sticks to the '*i* before e, except after c' rule. Just make sure you remember the *r*, or you'll have a fiend[9] instead, and no one wants that.

NECESSARY

If something is *necessary*, then it is very much needed. For example, food and water are *necessary* for humans to survive.

Spellcheck

Necessary is not *necessarily* the easiest word to spell, so you may find it *necessary* to remember this little hint: *necessary* has one c and two s's, so it's just like a shirt, which has one **c**ollar and two **s**leeves.

VACUUM

A *vacuum* can be a totally empty space of nothingness without any air in it, or it can mean to clean something up with a *vacuum cleaner*. Let's hope when you do the *vacuuming* your floor is a nice empty space afterwards.

---

[9] A fiend is someone who is really cruel and mean.

Other uses

A *vacuum flask* is a drinks container with double walls. The empty space between the walls helps to keep the flask's contents either hot or cold.

Spellcheck

Vacuum is a really unusual word in that it has one c followed by a double u. It comes from the Latin *vacuus*, which means 'empty'.

ARCTIC

The area around the North Pole is called the *Arctic*. The Antarctic is the area around the South Pole. Try not to get them mixed up!

Spellcheck

Watch out for the c in the middle of *Arctic*. If you miss that out, you'll have 'artic', which is a word for a type of truck.

Other uses

Arctic can also mean very cold.

Did you know?

You might think a penguin would make a nice snack for a polar bear, but in actual fact the two creatures would never meet in the wild. That's because polar bears live in the *Arctic,* and penguins live in the Antarctic.

LAUGH

If you find something funny, you'll probably *laugh* out loud, just like this: HA HA HA HEE HEE HOOOO! You get the idea.

Spellcheck

Spelling *laugh* is no *laughing* matter. It's not 'laff' and definitely not 'larf'. Just remember the *augh* part like this: laugh **a**nd **u** **g**et **h**appy!

EXTRA TOUGH TO SPELL

Words to leave even champion spellers cowering with fear.

MNEMONIC

You might not have realized it, but there are loads of *mnemonics* in this book. A *mnemonic* is a sentence, rhyme or system that helps you remember something – such as how to spell a word. Using '**b**ig **e**lephants **a**ren't **u**gly' to help you spell the first part of '**bea**utiful' is a mnemonic. So is '**o**h **u** lucky **d**uck' for remembering how to spell the end of **could**. One of the best-known *mnemonics* is '*i* before *e*, except after *c*'.

Silence please

Mnemonic looks like a real tongue-twister, until you discover that the first *m* is silent. So it's pronounced 'neh-maw-nick'.

Spellcheck

A *mnemonic* for *mnemonic*? You **may** **never** remember how to spell it!

MILLENNIUM

A time period of 1,000 years is called a *millennium*. Our current *millennium* started in the year 2000, which most adults still remember. The one before that started in the year 1000, which no one remembers!

Spellcheck

Millennium has two *l*'s and two *n*'s (and, if you look at the beginning and end, two *m*'s too).

CONSCIENCE

Your *conscience* is your sense of right and wrong. If you do something that you know is morally wrong, and you feel bad about it afterwards, you might be said to be suffering from a *guilty conscience*.

Spellcheck

Conscience is pronounced 'kon-shunss'. To spell it, just remember to add *con* to *science*.

Did you know?

During times of war, a person who refuses to join the armed forces for moral or religious reasons is called a *conscientious objector*.

CONSCIOUS

If you are reading this, then you must be conscious. Conscious means you are awake and aware of what is going on around you. The opposite of *conscious* is *unconscious*, which is when you are asleep or have been knocked out.

Other uses

You can also make a *conscious decision*. This means you did something deliberately, after giving it a lot of thought.

Spellcheck

Conscious is pronounced 'kon-shuss', but the spelling is very different. However, if you split it up into three parts, it's easier to remember: *con-sci-ous*.

DYSLEXIA

Dyslexia is a condition that makes it extra difficult for a person to read and spell. People who have this condition are *dyslexic*.

Spellcheck

Dyslexia is pronounced 'dis-lek-see-ah'. It's a little ironic that the word *dyslexia* is so hard to spell, given its meaning.

HUMOROUS

If something is funny or makes you laugh, it can be called *humorous*.

Spellcheck

Humorous is spelled the same way in English all over the world, even though the word it is based on is not. In the UK they use the spelling *humour*, while in the USA it's *humor*.

Not to be confused with...

Humerus (the bone in your arm that goes from your shoulder to your elbow).

YACHT

A boat with a sail or motor is called a *yacht*. *Yachts* are often used for tourist trips or races.

Spellcheck

Yacht is pronounced 'yot', so it's a simple word to say, if not to spell. Its strange spelling may have been influenced by the Dutch word it came from: *jaghtschip,* meaning pirate ship.

HIERARCHY

When people are divided up into different ranks, it's called a *hierarchy*. A person's boss, for example, would be higher up in the *hierarchy* than them. People such as kings, queens, presidents and prime ministers are at the very top of their *hierarchies*.

Spellcheck

If you have studied the ancient Egyptians, you might notice that *hierarchy* has the same beginning as 'hieroglyph'. It's pronounced the same way – like 'hire' rather than 'here'. The full word is pronounced 'hi-uh-rah-kee'.

PRECOCIOUS

If a child has abilities or talents above what would be expected of them at their age, they might be described as precocious. For example, *Kayla was very precocious. She was doing science lessons aimed at children two years older than her.*

Spellcheck

Precocious is pronounced 'preh-koe-shuss', so the two *c*'s can be a little confusing. Try remembering them by reminding yourself that the word describes clever children.

Not to be confused with...

Precious (something valuable). *Precious* and *precocious* look and sound similar, but they mean completely different things.

SECRETARY

A *secretary* usually works in an office, and their job is to organize things, make business arrangements and answer the telephone.

Other uses

Confusingly, a *secretary* can also be the title given to a senior person in a club or political party.

Spellcheck

Secretary starts with *secret*, so try remembering: Shh! The **secre**t*ary* knows all the boss's **secret**s!

> ### Did you know?
> There's also an African bird called a *secretary bird*. It is a large bird of prey with very long legs, and is related to hawks and eagles.

SECReTARy bird

SOLDIER

Someone who serves in an army is called a *soldier*.

Spellcheck

The *d* in *soldier* is misleading, as the word is pronounced 'sole-jur'. This may help to remember the odd spelling: Sadly, sometimes *sol**di**er**s** **die*** in battle.

Other uses

In some places, a *soldier* is the word used for a thin strip of bread or toast, used to dip into the runny yolk of a soft-boiled egg.

Not to be confused with...

Solder (using heat to join two pieces of metal together).

CHAUFFEUR

A *chauffeur* is employed to drive a car for someone else. However, *chauffeur* could be used for anyone driving a car for another person. For example, *Dad said it wasn't his job to chauffeur us around any more.*

Where does it come from?

The word comes from the French *chauffer*, which means 'to heat'. You pronounce it 'shoh-fer'.

DEFINITELY

When something is done *definitely*, it is done with great certainty. For example, *The baby definitely doesn't like her food – she threw it all over the floor!*

Spellcheck

Sometimes people mistakenly replace the second *i* with an *a*. Thinking of this phrase may help you to avoid that error: **I** insist there is no *a* in *definitely*.

Not to be confused with...

Defiantly (to aggressively resist authority). These two words often get mixed up because of their similar spelling, but they mean very different things.

SACRILEGIOUS

If a person is disrespectful towards a religion or anything considered holy, they may be accused of being *sacrilegious*.

Spellcheck

You would probably expect this word to contain the same spelling as 'religious', but it doesn't. That's because *sacrilegious* comes from the word *sacrilege*, which refers to disrespect for anything sacred. Try thinking of it this way: sac**rile**gious has **rile** in the middle, and if you are *sacrilegious* you're likely to rile[10] people!

MISSPELL

If you *misspell* a word, then you spell it incorrectly. Hopefully this book will help you cut down on that problem!

Spellcheck

Misspell is 'miss spell' squashed together to make one word. Notice that one s has been removed. This mini rhyme might help you remember how it's done:

Miss Pell,

Will never **misspell.**

---

[10] To rile someone means to annoy or anger them.

ONOMATOPOEIA

The use of words that sound like the noise they make, such as 'buzz', 'hiss' and 'growl', is called *onomatopoeia* (pronounced 'on-oh-mat-oh-pee-ah'). You can find lots more examples below. Can you think of any others?

Onomatopoeic words

- bam
- bang
- bump
- clap

- crash
- cuckoo
- plop
- swoosh
- zing

Spellcheck

Onomatopoeia is one of the hardest words to spell. Try remembering that the vowels in the last section appear in the same order as they do in the word 'p**oe**tic**a**l'.

INGENIOUS

If something is *ingenious*, it has been cleverly or inventively created. *Ingenious* is also sometimes used to describe people, but it's more commonly used for machines, inventions or ideas. For example, *Thomas Edison's invention of the light bulb was ingenious.*

Spellcheck

Notice that *ingenious* is spelled differently from 'genius'. Ingenious has an *o* in the middle.

Ingenious v genius

If someone is particularly clever or skilful, you could say they are either ingenious or 'a

genius'. Here are a couple of examples of the two words in action:
- *Evan was said to be a musical genius – he could play four different musical instruments at the age of seven.*
- *Evan was ingenious enough to play four different musical instruments at the age of seven.*

ACCOMMODATE

If you *accommodate* someone it means you find them a place to stay, or find some space for them. You can also be *accommodating*, which means willing to do things to please others.

Spellcheck

It may help to remember that this is a long word – long enough to *accommodate* two *a*'s, two *o*'s, a double *c* and a double *m*.

IMMEDIATE

Something that happens at once and without any delay is *immediate*. For example, if someone breaks their leg, they need *immediate* medical attention. *Immediate* can also mean 'nearest'. For example, *The Peacock family are our immediate neighbours.*

Spellcheck

Immediate has two m's and an ate. So you could remember the spelling by thinking: **mum ate imm**ed*iate*ly.

PRIVILEGE

A *privilege* is a special advantage or right that a person or group of people have been given. That's why, if someone has a lot of money, they might be described as very *privileged*.

Other uses

If you get the opportunity to do something really brilliant, you might also describe that as a *privilege*. For example, *Martina had the great privilege of meeting her all-time favourite singer.*

Spellcheck

Privilege is pronounced 'prih-veh-ledge', but note that the spelling has 'lege' at the end rather than 'ledge'. The phrase 'It's a *privi***lege** to have **legs**' might help you to remember that.

WOW WORDS

Words you can impress your friends, family and teachers with.

SCRUPULOUS

If you are *scrupulous*, you believe in being honest and fair, and doing the right thing. A *scrupulous* person is said to have *scruples*. *Scruples* are reservations or thoughts that would prevent you from doing something morally wrong. If you have *no scruples*, you might be described as *unscrupulous*, which probably means you're not to be trusted!

Other uses

Scrupulous can also mean careful and precise.

*Simpler synonyms**

[* Synonyms are different words that share the same meaning.]

Good, moral, proper, attentive

RAMPAGE

A fast, aggressive movement through a place is a *rampage*. If you go *on the rampage*, you're rushing around and causing damage – so try not to *rampage*, as it's not a nice thing to do! For example, *The angry protestors rampaged through the streets.*

Simpler synonyms

Riot, charge, frenzy, storm

DILAPIDATED

If you ever see a building that has become ruined through age or neglect, you could call it *dilapidated*.

Simpler synonyms

Derelict, shabby, ramshackle

CACOPHONY

A *cacophony* is a horrible racket! Think of lots of car alarms going off at the same time, or the sounds of loads of drivers all beeping their car horns.

Where does it come from?

Cacophony comes from the Greek word kakophōnia, meaning 'bad sound'. The *phony* part means 'sound', which is why it also appears in 'symphony'.

Simpler synonyms

Noise, din, racket

EUPHORIC

Euphoric means intensely happy and excited. For example, *The marathon runner felt euphoric as she crossed the finish line.* The feeling of happiness that a euphoric person experiences is *called euphoria.*

Simpler synonyms

Delighted, joyful, ecstatic, jubilant, elated

ABYSMAL

Something absolutely terrible or appalling can be described as *abysmal.* For example, *The standard of hygiene in medieval times was abysmal.*

Other uses

Abysmal can also mean 'very deep'. An abyss is another word for a deep (or even bottomless) hole, so it makes sense, although it's pretty rare to hear *abysmal* used in this way nowadays.

Simpler synonyms

Horrible, horrendous, dreadful, awful, frightful

SALUBRIOUS

A *salubrious* place is agreeable and pleasant. A part of town where the houses are nice and the streets are clean could be described as *salubrious*. Being *salubrious* is also connected to good health. For example, *Georgia felt on top of the world after her stay at a salubrious yoga retreat.*

Where does it come from?

Salubrious takes its origin from the Latin salūs, which means 'health'.

Simpler synonyms

Healthy, pleasant, respectable, wholesome

GORGEOUS

If you find something very attractive, you might call it *gorgeous*. *Gorgeous* is like 'nice', but a lot better. People, things, clothes, colours – pretty much anything can be *gorgeous*. For example, *Anne said the sunrise that morning was gorgeous.*

Where does it come from?

Gorgeous comes from the Old French word *gorgias*, meaning 'elegant'.

Spellcheck

Try remembering that the first part is the word *gorge*, as in, *Zander likes to gorge on chocolate.* After that, it's just a case of adding *ous* on to the end.

Simpler synonyms

Beautiful, glorious, stunning

FEROCIOUS

A *ferocious* person is someone who is violent, brutal and angry. Battles, fights and arguments are sometimes described as *ferocious*, especially the particularly nasty ones. *Ferocious* is often used for dangerous animals, too. For example, *Crocodiles are excellent swimmers and ferocious killers.*

Other uses

Ferocious can also describe things that are extreme, rather than violent. For example, *There* were *ferocious winds during the storm*. An intense emotion could be described as ferocious, too. *Helen had a ferocious hatred of homework*. In fact, any powerful feeling or pain can be *ferocious*. *Ahmed had a ferocious headache*.

Simpler synonyms

Savage, fierce, cruel, intense, vicious

INCANDESCENT

Things that give out a lot of light when they are heated are *incandescent*. You can have *incandescent* light bulbs, for example. The lava that comes out of a volcano could be described as *incandescent*.

Other uses

Incandescent can mean very emotional or passionate. You can have an *incandescent* love for something – or an *incandescent* rage!

Simpler synonyms

Blazing, raging, angry, irate

BERSERK

If someone is wild and out of control, they could be described as *berserk*. People can go *berserk* with anger or *berserk* with excitement.

For example, *Kwame lost his temper and went berserk.*

Where does it come from?

Berserk has a very cool origin. The *berserkers* were Viking warriors, who used to work themselves into a frenzy before battle, before literally going *berserk* on their enemies.

Simpler synonyms

Manic, wild, hysterical, frenzied

ULTIMATE

Ultimate means at the end. This book's *ultimate* word is *ultimate!*

Other uses

Ultimate can also mean best or most important. For example, *Cheryl considered strawberry to be the ultimate ice-cream flavour.* Weirdly, it can also mean worst. For Cheryl, *getting strawberry ice cream all over her face was the ultimate shame.*

Simpler synonyms

Last, final, complete, summit

Did you know?

Penultimate means the second-to-last thing. The *penultimate* word in this book is berserk.

Did you know?

Penultimate means the second-to-last thing. The penultimate word in this book is herself.

The end

The finish
The completion
The termination
The finale
The climax
The close
The cessation
The conclusion

The end

Index

A

aardvark, *120*
abysmal, *279*
accommodate, *275*
acute, *226*
advice, *97*
advise, *97*
aerobic, *40*
aeroplane, *54*
affect, *108*
aggressive, *33*
aggro, *33*
airplane, *54*
aisle, *97*
al dente, *118*
alektorophobia, *195*
alfresco, *118*
algebra, *222*
allergy, *197*
ambiguous, *128*
anaerobic, *40*
ancient, *131*
anonymous, *128*
anterior, *185*
anthology, *164*

anthophobia, *195*
anthropophobia, *195*
antibiotic, *197*
anticlimax, *174*
antihero, *174*
appreciate, *32*
apprehensive, *62*
arachnophobia, *195*
arc, *228*
archaeology, *131*
architecture, *138*
arid, *218*
Arctic, *7, 260*
arithmetic, *222*
ark, *228*
artefact, *132*
asthma, *250*
atlas, *165*
atmosphere, *3*
attentive, *77*
autobiography, *165*
automobile, *181*
autonomy, *181*
avalanche, *220*
avatar, *120*

average, *224*
aw, *63*
awed, *63*

B

bafflegab, *241*
balderdash, *241*
ballad, *145*
ballet, *120*
bamboozle, *242*
bankrupt, *200*
barbecue, *20*
bare, *84*
bargain, *206*
barometer, *228*
base, *146*
bass, *146*
bear, *84*
beautiful, *256*
berserk, *285*
biannual, *171*
biceps, *190*
biodegradable, *14*
biography, *164*
biplane, *171*
biscuit, *120*
bluff, *120*
blunder, *120*
boar, *86*

boil, *20*
bore, *86*
bruise, *190*
burglary, *250*

C

cacophony, *279*
café, *120*
calendar, *256*
campaign, *40*
cancel, *185*
canvas, *45*
canvass, *45*
catacomb, *113*
cauldron, *111*
cemetery, *113*
center, *53*
centre, *53*
chauffeur, *269*
cheap, *206*
cheep, *206*
Chile, *94*
chili, *94*
chilli, *94*
chilly, *94*
chit, *120*
chord, *146*
chorophobia, *195*
chorus, *143*

circumference, *228*
climate, *211*
climax, *174, 211*
codswallop, *239*
coexist, *179*
coffee, *120*
coffin, *114*
collage, *159*
college, *159*
collywobbles, *234*
colonel, *99*
committee, *50*
communicate, *68*
community, *50*
competition, *36*
complement, *93*
compliment, *93*
composer, *148*
conductor, *148*
conker, *133*
conquer, *133*
conscience, *263*
conscious, *263*
consensus, *247*
continent, *7*
controversy, *33*
convenience, *209*
cookie, *120*
cord, *146*

correspond, *76*
coughing, *114*
could, *247*
council, *50*
counsel, *50*
coup, *45*
coworker, *179*
criticize, *71*
croissant, *120*
crypt, *113*
curiosity, *63*
curious, *63*
currant, *17*
currency, *205*
current, *17*
cute, *226*
cymbal, *153*

D

dear, *88*
decathlon, *36*
decipher, *170*
decline, *170*
deer, *88*
defiantly, *269*
definitely, *269*
dehydration, *197*
delicatessen, *120*
democracy, *40*

deposit, *200*
depressed, *63*
desert, *103*
desperate, *62*
dessert, *103*
determined, *63*
dialog, *59*
dialogue, *59*
diameter, *228*
diarrhoea, *197*
dictatorship, *40*
dictionary, *161*
diddly-squat, *238*
diet, *14*
difficulty, *250*
dilapidated, *279*
dim sum, *120*
disastrous, *29*
discombobulate, *234*
discount, *206*
dissect, *176*
dissimilar, *176*
doe, *20*
doppelgänger, *236*
dough, *20*
dribble, *36*
drizzle, *212*
drought, *214*
dynasty, *136*

dyslexia, *264*

E

eavesdrop, *76*
economy, *50*
eerie, *114*
effect, *108*
egghead, *234*
election, *40*
embarrass, *247*
empire, *136*
encyclopedia, *163*
ensemble, *149*
entrepreneur, *120*
environment, *2*
equator, *4*
espresso, *118*
euphoric, *279*
exaggerate, *69*
excellent, *29*
exchange, *205*
explain, *69*
eyrie, *114*

F

favorite, *60*
favourite, *60*
ferocious, *283*
fiction, *164*
fiddlesticks, *242*

fiend, *256*
finite, *232*
fir, *88*
flea, *90*
flee, *90*
fog, *214*
foreign, *9*
foul, *89*
fowl, *89*
fractious, *194*
fracture, *194*
friend, *256*
fruit, *17*
fry, *20*
fur, *88*
futile, *128*

G

gargoyle, *241*
gazump, *242*
genes, *99*
genius, *275*
genuphobia, *195*
geothermal, *14*
glitch, *120*
gobbledegook, *234*
gorgeous, *282*
gorilla, *45*
government, *40*
grate, *20*
great, *20*
grill, *20*
guarantee, *209*
guerrilla, *45*
gung-ho, *120*
guru, *120*
guttersnipe, *239*

H

Halloween, *109*
harass, *71*
heal, *93*
heard, *86*
heel, *93*
he'll, *93*
heptathlon, *36*
herd, *86*
hierarchy, *266*
him, *153*
horizon, *9*
humerus, *264*
humid, *218*
humorous, *264*
hurricane, *215*
hymn, *153*
hysterical, *63*

I

I'll, *97*

immediate, *276*
incandescent, *283*
incontinent, *7*
index, *165*
indict, *250*
indite, *250*
infinite, *232*
ingenious, *275*
injury, *188*
insincere, *79*
insipid, *29*
interfere, *70*
interrupt, *70*
island, *7*
isle, *97*
isobar, *220*
isohyet, *220*
isotherm, *220*

J

jargon, *234*
jeans, *99*
jewellery, *54*
jewelry, *54*

K

karaoke, *120*
kawaii, *120*
kernel, *99*
kindergarten, *120*

klutz, *120*
knead, *20*
kosher, *120*
kung fu, *120*

L

landscape, *156*
language, *68*
laugh, *260*
lemon, *120*
liaison, *253*
licence, *59*
license, *59*
lightening, *218*
lightning, *218*
loan, *200*
lobby, *45*
lone, *200*
lyrics, *142*

M

macabre, *116*
maneuver, *59*
manoeuvre, *59*
marathon, *36*
marvellous, *29*
mausoleum, *113*
medal, *102*
meddle, *102*
medieval, *132*

medium, *159*
meerkat, *120*
melody, *145*
metropolis, *128*
millennium, *262*
millionaire, *253*
mint, *200*
minuscule, *246*
mischievous, *29*
misfit, *172*
mishap, *172*
missed, *214*
misshapen, *172*
misspell, *269*
mist, *214*
mnemonic, *262*
monotonous, *77*
monsoon, *212*
muscle, *190*
mussel, *190*

N
naval, *192*
navel, *192*
necessary, *256*
need, *20*
nephophobia, *195*
network, *82*
non-fiction, *164*

North Pole, *4*
nuisance, *29*

O
observe, *157*
obtuse, *226*
occurrence, *247*
octophobia, *195*
offence, *54*
offense, *54*
Olympics, *35*
onomatopoeia, *269*
operation, *231*
optimistic, *63*
orchestra, *148, 149, 151*
organic, *10*
origami, *120*

P
pajamas, *57*
paleontologist, *131*
paparazzi, *118*
papyrophobia, *195*
Paralympics, *35*
paraplegic, *195*
pastime, *247*
patio, *120*
peace, *105*
penultimate, *285*
pepperoni, *118*

percent, *223*
percussion, *151*
periwinkle, *242*
persuade, *81*
pescatarian, *17*
pessimistic, *63*
petrify, *111*
pharaoh, *136*
phenomenal, *32*
phenomenon, *32*
phobia, *128, 195*
phobophobia, *195*
physical, *188*
pi, *232*
pie, *232*
piece, *105*
piñata, *120*
pitch, *145*
plausible, *128*
pogonophobia, *195*
pole, *4*
poll, *4, 244*
polliwog, *244*
pollution, *2*
portcullis, *138*
portrait, *156*
posterior, *185*
postpone, *185*
practice, *60*

practise, *60*
precede, *184*
precious, *266*
precipitation, *212*
precocious, *266*
predict, *184*
prehistoric, *129*
prejudice, *81*
prime, *231*
principal, *105*
principle, *105*
privilege, *276*
profit, *108*
program, *54*
programme, *54*
pronounce, *79*
prophet, *108*
pterodactyl, *255*
pyjamas, *57*

R
radius, *228*
ragamuffin, *239*
ragga, *239*
rain, *102*
rampage, *277*
ransack, *120*
rapport, *82*
recommend, *74*

recyclable, *12*
referendum, *40*
refund, *206*
reign, *102*
rein, *102*
renewable, *12*
restaurant, *14*
reusable, *12*
rhyme, *141*
rhythm, *141*
rile, *269*
roast, *20*
rucksack, *120*

S

sacrilegious, *269*
safari, *120*
salary, *204*
salivating, *14*
salubrious, *282*
sambal, *153*
schedule, *246*
schlep, *120*
schmooze, *120*
score, *142*
scrupulous, *277*
sculpt, *155*
secretary, *266*
self-portrait, *156*

separate, *250*
siesta, *120*
sincere, *79*
sketch, *155*
sketchy, *155*
skulduggery, *244*
solder, *269*
soldier, *269*
solo, *145*
South Pole, *4*
spaghetti, *26*
spectre, *116*
speech, *82*
spine, *165*
spook, *120*
state, *10*
stationary, *106*
stationery, *106*
stomach, *192*
submarine, *178*
suburb, *178*
suffrage, *137*
suggest, *74*
supernatural, *116*
sustainable, *14*
symbol, *153*
symmetry, *224*
symphony, *149*
symptom, *194*

synonym, *161, 277*

T

tacks, *204*
tactics, *36*
tambourine, *151*
tax, *204*
their, *96*
there, *96*
thermometer, *228*
thesaurus, *161*
they're, *96*
tomb, *113*
tone, *157*
tornado, *215*
translate, *182*
transmit, *182*
traveler, *57*
traveller, *57*
trek, *120*
trivial, *29*
trophy, *36*
tropic, *4*
Tropic of Cancer, *4*
Tropic of Capricorn, *4*
tsunami, *216*
typhoon, *216*

U

ultimate, *285*
umami, *26*
umlaut, *236*
unicorn, *187*
university, *187*

V

vacuum, *256*
vamoose, *238*
vegan, *17*
vegetable, *17*
vegetarian, *17*
verse, *143*
versus, *143*
voyage, *132*

W

wage, *204*
warlock, *116*
warranty, *209*
wear, *84*
weather, *106*
where, *84*
whether, *106*
who's, *89*
whose, *89*
wicked, *27*
widdershins, *238*
winkle-picker, *242*
Winter Olympics, *35*
wok, *120*

Y

yacht, *266*
your, *96*
you're, *96*
Yule, *120*

www.ingramcontent.com/pod-product-compliance
Lightning Source LLC
Chambersburg PA
CBHW011305150426
43191CB00016B/2343